MOROCCO

— in your pocket —

MICHELIN

MAIN CONTRIBUTOR: JAMES KEEBLE
PHOTOGRAPH CREDITS
Photos supplied by The Travel Library: A Birkett 22, 92;
Stuart Black 7, 8, 11, 13, 14, 17, 18 (left), 40, 42, 46, 51,
52, 54, 56 (bottom), 63, 66, 69, 72, 76, 81, 96, 99, 100,
105, 114; Stephanie Colasanti title page, 102, 108; James
Davis Travel Photography 26, 28, 30, 31, 41, 44; Lee
Frost 78, 80, 88, 91; John R Jones back cover, 4, 56
(top), 68, 75, 83, 106; Darren Lewey 79; Guy Marks 111;
M Simon Matthews 35; Christine Osborne front cover,
21, 24, 38, 39, 59, 60, 65, 87; Grant Pritchard 18 (right),
32, 37, 71, 103, 113, 121, 123; Simon Reddy 67;
R Richardson 45, 48; Ian Robinson 74 (inset, main), 94,
116, 119; David Rose 124.
Other photos: Nature Photographers WS Paton 61;
Roger Tidman 84.

*Front cover: Koutoubia Minaret, Marrakech; back cover: Erg
Chebbi dunes, Merzouga; title page: dyers' souk, Marrakech*

MANUFACTURE FRANÇAISE DES PNEUMATIQUES MICHELIN

Société en commandite par actions au capital de 2 000 000 000 de francs

Place des Carmes-Déchaux – 63 Clermont-Ferrand (France)

R.C.S. Clermont-Fd 855 200 507

© Michelin et Cie. Propriétaires-Éditeurs 1997

Dépôt légal Mai 97 – ISBN 2-06-651401-2 – ISSN en cours

Printed in Spain 7-97

CONTENTS

INTRODUCTION

A land of epic history, a land of exceptional diversity, Morocco will both intrigue and inspire the visitor. It lies on the northernmost tip of the vast continent of Africa, yet it is just 14km (9 miles) across the

The imposing dunes of Erg Chebbi, at Merzouga, are particularly stunning.

Straits of Gibraltar to Europe. Morocco is a country renowned for its warm welcome, sun-drenched landscapes and enduring mystery.

Contrasts abound in this immense country. Its long western coast is washed by the crashing waves of the Atlantic Ocean, while to the north the warm Mediterranean caresses its shores. Inland, the traveller can experience the exhilarating views while trekking in the high mountain ranges, or indulge in the eery solitude of the vast expanses of desert. There are fertile plains and plateaus, dramatic valleys running down from the mountains and arid areas interspersed with brights splashes of the oases.

As if the variety of landscapes were not enough, Morocco offers a rich combination of cultures, people and architecture. Here, the sophisticated culture of the Arab world blends with the raw beauty of Africa. It has unique cities in which imperial architecture and medieval souks provide a glimpse of traditions that have changed little during the last thousand years. Great universities and mosques remind the visitor of the splendour of the Berber Islamic empires, while the new business districts of Casablanca and Rabat point to a new future for the kingdom, as King Hassan II prepares to lead his people into the next millennium.

Yet despite these ambitions, and the increasing development of mass tourism, Morocco will still surprise, with its ever-shifting mix of the ancient and modern, the Arab and the African. It is a land that is sure to charm and intrigue those who explore the rich and varied experiences held in store here.

GEOGRAPHY

Since the great Arab warrior Oqba ibn Nafi first rode his white horse right into the surf of the Atlantic, claiming the territory for Allah, Morocco has been known as Maghreb-el-Aksa, 'the land farthest west'. It is a country of extremes, from the fertile shores of the Mediterranean to the barren endless sands of the Sahara.

Morocco is vast. Its territory, some 710 850 sq km (274 460 sq miles), is three times the size of Great Britain and larger than Texas. It is also one of the most mountainous countries in Africa, with 15 per cent of the landmass soaring over 2 000m (6 500ft). It is characterised by its geographical diversity, from the Mediterranean and Atlantic coasts, to mountain ranges including the third highest mountain in Africa, lush fertile plains and, further south, the first sands of the Sahara desert.

In the north, the Mediterranean extends 530km (330 miles) to Algeria, a coastline composed of cliffs and coves. The landscape is mountainous, resembling more the southern coast of France than any African vista. The **Rif mountains** are immensely fertile, due to a healthy rainfall.

Further south are three ranges of mountains extending from west to east. The **Middle Atlas** (Moyen Atlas) consist of high, partially-forested plateaus, populated by semi-nomadic Berber tribes. The **High Atlas** (Haut Atlas) mountains are the most dramatic, and boast some of the highest peaks in Africa, including 400 peaks over 3 000m (9 850ft). Three passes cross the mountain range, only one of which – the Tizi-n-Babaou – is passable in winter. At one

time the Berber tribes from the High Atlas descended to the plains in winter, moving up into the mountains during the summer. By the 19C most of the Berber tribes had been expelled from the plains by the Arabs and many Berbers took up residence in the highlands. The parched smaller mountains of the **Anti-Atlas**, punctuated with green oases, mark the beginning of the southern desert areas.

From the northern Cap Spartel, outside Tangier, 2 800km (1 736 miles) of **Atlantic coast** run south to Mauritania – one long beach backed by sand dunes. The Atlantic is fed by two majestic rivers, the Oum er-Rbia and Oued Sebou, which irrigate the wide, flat **central plains** of western Morocco.

The Ourika Valley cuts into the High Atlas mountains.

These fertile plains form the main agricultural region of Morocco. More specialised fruit farms are being developed to supply the European market during cold winter months, as well as flower exportation businesses. The land lying eastwards to the Algerian border is far less hospitable, a barren **steppe region** merging gradually into the Sahara.

Past the Anti-Atlas mountains, water all but disappears as the landscape turns to desert – not the sand dunes of classic fairy stories, but flat and rocky *hammada*, the stone-baked desert of southern Morocco. The real gems of the southern scenery are the overwhelmingly fertile oases that follow the rare river beds, necklaces of greenery between the dusty rocks.

The Roman city of Volubilis is Morocco's finest archaeological site.

HISTORY

Early Invasions

Near southern Akka, rock drawings have been found that date back to around 3000BC, evidence of a **Neolithic** culture that thrived in the caves of the Anti-Atlas mountains. Morocco's strategic position at the gateway to the Mediterranean meant that development along its coast began with the onset of sea-travel. From 1200-500BC, **Phoenician** trading posts were established along the coast, trading in gold, corn and pottery. This period also saw the growth of Carthage in Tunisia until, inevitably, the **Romans** destroyed the city in 146BC and assumed the protectorate over the former Phoenician colonies. They controlled an area including both Morocco (primarily the north-western coastal region, extending south to Rabat) and eastern Algeria, which was known as Mauretania. The Romans so liked the Moroccan extent of this territory, Mauretania Tingitana, that they built the city of **Volubilis**, near Meknès – a fantastic metropolis of temples, markets and houses which still survives to this day. Roman influence spread throughout Morocco, but it was a constant struggle as the legions attempted to quell the local Berber tribes.

When the Romans withdrew in the second half of the 3C, Morocco was divided up into local Berber fiefdoms. Yet this beautiful and fertile land continued to attract foreign interest: the **Vandals** sent raiding parties to take slaves and gold and to exploit the local resources, and attempted to rule North Africa for a century until the **Byzantines** defeated them in the 6C.

BACKGROUND

Islamic Rule

It was an invasion in 683 that defined the future of Morocco. From the east came a marauding Arab army, led by **Oqba ibn Nafi**, whose mission was to conquer an empire for Islam. After founding the city of Kairouan (south of Tunis) and building the first mosque in Africa, he swept into Morocco, reaching as far as the Atlantic coast. The Berbers put up a fierce resistance, and Oqba ibn Nafi was killed while on his return journey at Biskra. A turbulent period followed, but when **Moussa ibn Nasr** launched another attack in 703, he succeeded in quelling the Berbers, and enlisted their best warriors for a successful assault on Spain.

So Morocco became Arab, and played its part in the intrigues that were besetting the Arab world. In 788 **Idriss I**, a powerful *sherif* (descendant of the Prophet) exiled from Baghdad following the Sunni-Shiite split in Islam, was welcomed in Volubilis and named ruler by local Berber tribes, establishing the first Arab dynasty in Morocco – the **Idrissids**. The Caliph of Baghdad, sensing a rival force growing in the west, sent agents to Morocco who poisoned Idriss I. His son, **Moulay Idriss II**, became one of the greatest leaders in Moroccan history, founding the majestic city of **Fès**, and expanding the territory to include much of present-day Morocco. By the time of Moulay Idriss II's death in 829, he had established a strong stable state. However, the kingdom was then divided among his nine sons, and the power of the state was diluted and vulnerable to powerful neighbouring dynasties.

A new force emerged from Berber tribes in the south. The Almoravid leader **Youssef**

ibn Tashfin swept northwards, conquering territory as far as Spain and founding his own capital, **Marrakech**, in 1062. Using the city as their base, the Almoravids expanded northwards, taking Fès and the remainder of the Idrissid kingdom. By 1080 they had extended as far east as Algiers. By the time of his death, at over 100 years old, Youssef ibn Tashfin had established a stable and prosperous kingdom. His son, Ali, and the three rulers who followed him were less effective, and were unable to contain the tough Berber leaders as discontent gradually spread.

As Morocco became increasingly secular, trade links were established with Europe and lands to the south. In the mid-12C this development of trade and ideas was called into question by **Ibn Toumert**, a strict theologian preaching a return to Islamic fundamentalism. This new Berber dynasty, the **Almohads**, brought in the golden age of Moroccan religious architecture, including the Koutoubia in Marrakech and Tour Hassan (Hassan Tower) in Rabat.

A monument to the golden age of Almohad architecture – the unfinished Hassan Tower, Rabat, and the columns of what was planned to be the largest mosque in the world.

The Christian Influence

In Europe the Pope, anxious about the increasing power of Islam, sent a huge Christian army to challenge the Almohads, who were defeated at Las Navas de Tolosa, in Spain, in 1212. This defeat led to a new dynasty emerging in Morocco, the **Merenids**, who originated from southern desert Berber tribes. Their rule was one of relative calm, during which the arts, religious study and architecture flourished.

This peace did not last. Former advisors to the Merenid rulers rebelled in 1465 and yet another dynasty was formed, the **Wattasids**, who presided over a period of great unrest during which Spain and Portugal established bases along the coast.

With Morocco and Islamic territories in disarray, the Spanish Christians were at last able to seize Granada in 1492, ending 700 years of Islamic rule in Andalusia. The Spanish inquisition began, and Muslim and Jewish refugees fled to Moroccan cities. It was time to regroup and consolidate, and in 1554 the powerful southern *marabouts* (holy warriors) banded together to form the **Saadian** dynasty and drive out the Spanish and Portuguese. Their new sultan, **Ahmed El Mansour**, developed relations with Europe and conquered lands as far as Timbuktu.

The Alaouite Dynasty

The present-day Alaouite dynasty, descendants from the Prophet, emerged from Rissani in the south. The first Alaouite Sultan, Moulay Rachid, was invited to Fès to assume the throne of Morocco in 1668. He was succeeded on his death, in 1672, by his younger brother **Moulay Ismaïl**. A ruthless leader, aided by an army of 150 000 African slaves, Moulay Ismaïl has earned the reputation of being a harsh, tyrannical leader. Despite his acts of cruelty, he can be credited with creating stability and uniting even the most isolated parts of the country. He founded his own capital, Meknès, forced the British and Spanish to retreat from the coast and even attempted to marry the daughter of French King Louis XIV. By 1750, the state was well established, and was one of the first countries to recognise the fledgling United States of America, beginning a close relationship that persists to this day.

In the 19C, Morocco's independence

waned once more. In 1880, the Madrid Conference established European control of Tangier, dividing the city between colonial powers. At the turn of the century the country was left bankrupt and French troops landed at Casablanca and Oujda. In 1912, the **Treaty of Fès** granted France *Maroc Utile* – 'useful Morocco' – while Spain received territory in the far south. Tangier, in turn, was declared an International Zone, and grew notorious for its international parties and social intrigue.

Morocco was early to support the Allies during the Second World War, hosting an historic conference between Churchill and Roosevelt in Casablanca. **Mohammed V**'s demands for independence were finally realised after the war, in 1956.

Mounted guard outside the Mausoleum of Mohammed V, Rabat.

Modern Morocco
With the death of Mohammed V in 1961, his
son **Hassan II** succeeded to the throne and
set about an ambitious programme of
modernisation. In 1975, he led 350 000

The vast Hassan II Mosque, on the shores of the Atlantic, Casablanca.

civilians south into the desert to claim the Western Sahara from Spain, in what became know as the **Green March**. This began ten years of guerrilla war with Algerian-backed Polisario fighters seeking independent territory in the Western Sahara, until a peace accord was finally signed in 1989.

During the **Gulf War** of 1990-1991, Morocco sent 1 300 troops to defend Kuwait, leading to pro-Iraqi riots in major cities, which had a devastating effect on the tourist industry. Saudi Arabia subsequently wrote off a $2 billion debt. The following year, the long-awaited Western Sahara referendum was postponed by UN observers, for fear of vote-rigging.

In 1993, a new Moroccan parliament was installed. The new sense of unity in the country was enhanced with the opening of the **Hassan II Mosque** in Casablanca, a vast edifice paid for largely by public subscription.

Despite its position on the edge of a troubled area, modern Morocco is a stable country, whose geographical position just a few miles from Europe makes it an important link with Africa and the Arab world. There are still major problems facing the nation's attempts to modernise, not least of which are the disparity between the wealth and industry concentrated in the major cities and the poverty of the countryside, unemployment and a high illiteracy rate.

However, the determination of the nation to move forward into the 21C is strong, and this, together with income from the tourism industry, may help to overcome these internal difficulties.

THE PEOPLE AND CULTURE

Morocco is a confident and welcoming country, with twelve centuries of history as a single national entity. The legacy of Moroccan sultans in the Western Mediterranean is evident in the country's fabulous architectural heritage. Today, the country enjoys a reputation as one of the most hospitable in the Arab world.

Morocco's heritage is diverse. The indigenous inhabitants were the **Berbers** – a people whose origins are not known for certain but who are thought to have come from ancient Libya. Speaking their own language, Berbers are found in many parts of North Africa but over sixty per cent live in Morocco. With the onset of Arab settlement in the 7C-8C, many Berber tribes became 'Arabized' and moved to the new cities, creating a social mix that has formed Morocco's character. Today, most Berbers speak both Arabic and one of the many Berber dialects. Berber tribes in the more remote areas, particularly in the High Atlas, have retained their traditional culture, and many speak little Arabic or French (*see* p.75). Although Arabic is the official language, most Moroccans speak some French (a legacy of the Protectorate), and it is taught in schools and is the language of higher education, government and major industry in the cities.

The Arabs converted the Berbers to **Islam**, which still plays an important role in Moroccan society today, with most Moroccans being Muslim (Sunnite). Even the smallest villages have a local mosque (*jemma* in Arabic), from which the call to prayer is sung five times a day by the *muezzin*,

Traditional water-seller.

at dawn, noon, mid-afternoon, dusk and mid-evening. Friday is the Islamic holy day, when a congregational prayer is offered at noon. In Morocco, entry to nearly all mosques is prohibited to non-Muslims.

Perhaps due to its distance from the centre of orthodox Islam, Morocco has always tolerated popular spiritualism. Many Moroccans still believe in the curative and inspirational powers of *marabouts*, the tombs of local holy men which are held in great awe. Religious fervour is acute in rural areas, and non-Muslims are advised to keep away from such tombs.

King Hassan II has sought to craft a unique blend of traditional Islamic practice and modern economic development. As a direct descendant of Mohammed, his role as a spiritual as well as political leader has

Muslim women wearing the traditional veil and hijab (headcovering).

enabled him thus far to maintain a comfortable balance, and the violent fundamentalism witnessed by Algeria has been avoided in Morocco.

Traditionally, **women** have been second-class citizens in Moroccan society. Islamic law states that while a man may have four wives, a woman can only have one husband. Yet today, most Moroccan marriages are monogamous, and women are beginning to find a voice. In the big cities, women conduct their lives and careers much as in any Western city. Birth rates have halved, thanks to the widespread availability of birth control, and girls are now receiving an education comparable to that of boys. As King Hassan has said: 'All paths are open to Moroccan women and they must take these paths.' The first Summit for European and Mediterranean Women was hosted by Morocco (in Marrakech in 1994), indicating that the country is ready to take up this challenge.

ART AND ARCHITECTURE

Islamic Influences

Moroccan art and architecture are inherently connected to Islam. According to Koranic edicts, the first ever mosque was built by Mohammed, in Medina. Mosque means literally 'a place of prostration', and they are always oriented towards Mecca, Mohammed's birthplace. This direction is marked by the *mihrab,* the prayer niche from where the *imam* leads prayer. The forecourt, the *sahn,* contains a pool and fountain in which worshippers wash themselves before prayer. The call to prayer, issued by a muezzin five times a day, is sounded out from the minaret. Moroccan minarets tend to be square, unlike the round towers found in more eastern Islamic countries.

Islam forbids the use of images, but does permit intricate decoration. The *medersas* (religious schools devoted to the study of the Koran and Islam) of Fès, Meknès and Marrakech boast fabulous stucco carving, colourful *zellij* mosaic decorations, and delicate calligraphy, to draw the eye from the world of man to the world of God. Black and white interlocking patterns can be seen lining the walls, symbolising the opposing forces of good and evil, while beneath them a verse from the Koran reads 'God is great. There is no God but God...'

Almost all building styles are influenced by the Koran. Small arches and arched gateways represent the arch of paradise. Gateways are a favourite feature of Moroccan homes, since in Islam heaven is guarded by seven gateways through which believers have to pass to reach God.

In a country in which graven images are forbidden by Islam, art has always been non-pictoral. Instead, artists have tended to be craftsmen, creating fabulous pottery, silverware, carpets, jewellery and woodwork.

Berber Architecture
The austere style of traditional Berber architecture contrasts with the highly-decorated, intricately carved interiors of Islamic buildings. The *agadirs* (fortified granaries), *kasbahs* (homes of local leader, with smaller homes clustered around it) and *ksour* (fortified castles or villages) are constructed from ochre-coloured defensive lower walls, with baked brick walls above. Despite their forbidding appearance, the baked mud from which they are built does not always stand the test of time against the elements.

Western Influences
The French chose to build outside the old medinas, creating towns reminiscent of Europe in the 1930s, with Casablanca boasting some interesting Art Deco buildings. The Moorish influence of Spain

Detail of the fine decorative carved woodwork in the Medersa Bou Inania.

has integrated more subtly in the architecture, in the form of rich geometric, floral and calligraphic decorative elements.

In the 19C and 20C, French influences have led to a small school of Moroccan painters, drawn by the exotic and oriental setting, the relaxed way of life, and the quality of the light. Tangier attracted such eminent artists as Eugene Delacroix, Kees Van Dongen, Henri Matisse, Albert Marquet and Francis Bacon. Asilah today hosts an international arts festival, and in Essaouira artists display their vibrant, colourful paintings interpreting female emancipation in Morocco.

MUST SEE

Fès★★★

A city of such unique architecture and atmosphere that UNESCO has declared it a World Heritage Site, Fès is, above all, supremely Arab, a place where refinement and chaos go hand in hand.

Marrakech★★★

Arch-rival to Fès, Marrakech with its exotic African character is the the gateway to the south. Its great square, the celebrated Jemaa el Fna, is a carnival of sights, sound and smells, and its oases and gardens will seduce even the most sight-weary traveller.

The huge, vibrant Jemaa el Fna forms the heart of Marrakech.

Rabat★★★

Morocco's administrative capital, Rabat is a French-designed cosmopolitan city with grand architecture, including the Mausoleum of Mohammed V, the mystic Chellah Gardens and the Kasbah des Oudaïas, overlooking the Atlantic.

Tafraoute★★★

Tafraoute, with its picturesque baked-mud houses, sits on the slopes of the Anti-Atlas mountains, above fertile valleys.

Drâa Valley Drive★★

This beautiful drive takes you from the desert outpost of Ouarzazate to the very edge of the Sahara, along the bed of the Drâa river and its thousand oases, where crocodiles once roamed.

Tangier★★

While Fès is Arab and Marrakech African, Tangier is European. Facing the Rock of Gibraltar, this former international playground is now a growing tourist resort, with white beaches and vast hotel blocks, yet the chaotic fervour of the kasbah and the maze of narrow streets of the medina have a charm all their own.

Essaouira★★

One of the more enchanting towns in Morocco, Essaouira is an exquisite fishing port, and home to some of the best windsurfing beaches in Africa.

Meknès★★

Sultan Moulay Ismaïl's capital is a monument to imperial glory, with the most impressive defensive walls in the country.

Chefchaouen★★

A small, charming town in the wild Rif mountains, painted white and little touched by mass tourism.

Dadès Valley★★

Follow the course of the Dadès river as it cuts through the High Atlas to form a dramatic gorge, contrasting with the broad, fertile oasis valley of the lower reaches of the river, peppered with delightful kasbahs, 'the valley of a thousand kasbahs'.

THE NORTH

Separated from Europe by the thinnest stretch of water, the north of Morocco is far from the stereotyped barren image people may have of North Africa. The Mediterranean coastline is as green and mountainous as the French Riviera, while the white sand beaches are reminiscent of the Greek islands. Once this was a wild land of bandits and warrior tribes, but successions of invading armies have never managed to tame its extreme landscapes and ferocious inhabitants.

Today, tourism is the region's number one industry and new hotel and apartment complexes are being built along the exquisite coast, resorts to rival anything the rest of the Mediterranean can offer.

The focus of the region is, of course, the great growing port of Tangier, one-time international playground and the gateway between two continents. Further east, lie two geographical anomalies – the Spanish enclaves of Ceuta and Melilla – while on the border with Algeria stands Oujda, a city that has been much fought over in the past because of its strategic position.

TANGIER (Tanger)

Tangier has always been a city apart from the rest of Morocco. Its history has been one of foreign occupation. European powers have long envied the city's strategic position at the entrance to the Mediterranean; the first invaders were the Romans, followed by a succession of European powers over the last 2 000 years, including Portuguese, British and French. In 1923 an international authority was set up, and Tangier was controlled by a

Tangier's strategic position at the western entrance to the Mediterranean has been coveted through the ages.

combination of nations, including France, Britain, Spain, Portugal and Italy. The lax regulations meant that licentiousness and illicit activities were tolerated here, and it became a centre for smuggling, political intrigue and dubious trading activites. In its 1920s heyday it was considered the most international city in the world, a place where numerous writers, artists and socialites met to indulge in activities forbidden in most other countries.

Modern Tangier is a long way from the crazy fleshpot of the 1920s. Today it is a relaxed city, a modern port, with a growing

Buying daily provisions at Tangier's busy market.

tourist trade. The nightspots that made its name are now long closed, and its less reputable image endures only in the tall tales of tourist guides. Yet it remains a vibrant metropolis, with a mysterious kasbah, long sandy beaches and wide, colonial boulevards.

Any visit to Tangier will usually begin at the city's main square, the **Grand Socco** (Place 9 Avril 1947). Its second name was added to mark Sultan Mohammed's appearance in the square to call for Moroccan independence from France. 'Socco' comes from *souk*, meaning 'market'. The square is still a lively meeting place, crammed with scooters, cars and carts. Riffians still descend from the Rif mountains to market on Thursdays and Sundays, dressed in traditional wide sombreros, but without their camels and muskets. A large blue door on the western side of the square leads to the **Jardins de la Mendoubia** (Mendoubia Gardens), containing the immense 800-year-old Dragon Tree. If you look carefully at the gnarled and twisted trunk you may be able to make out the figure of a man. According to legend, the tree captured the spirit of a wicked 13C prince who remains trapped in the tree.

Medina

From the Grand Socco you can access the medina via **Rue des Siaghines**, the one-time jewellers' street, now housing T-shirt stalls. This street leads to the **Petit Socco★**, the heart of the medina, and thus the heart of Tangier. It was visited by many writers and artists, from Francis Bacon to the American writers Paul Bowles, William Burroughs and Tennessee Williams. The square was once

the most fashionable meeting place in the city, patronised by artists like Raoul Dufy and Henri Matisse, and movie stars such as Errol Flynn and Cary Grant. Their favourite café, the **Café Central**, still survives today, albeit in a state of graceful disrepair.

In the northern corner of the medina lies the most celebrated landmark in Tangier, the infamous **kasbah**. This 17C fortified district of the medina was popular with foreigners – Woolworth heiress Barbara Hutton lived in the vast palace of Villa Sidi Hosni. The people of Tangier so liked the bubbly heiress that they permitted the widening of the kasbah streets to allow her Rolls Royce to pass by. Today, it is still one of the most desirable residential areas, with modern mansions in traditional style blending in with the older buildings. The **Place de la Kasbah** is the highest point, offering **views★** across the city to Gibraltar and Spain.

The Bab el Assa gate leads to the **Dar el Makhzen★★** (Royal Palace), built by Moulay Ismaïl to celebrate the English departure from Tangier in 1684. It now contains the **Musée ethnographique et archéologique★** (Archaeology and Ethnography Museum) displaying Roman artefacts, pottery, beautiful mosaics, illuminated Korans and a collection of rugs. Next door, the **Sultan's Gardens** provide a green and leafy haven within the hectic medina. Crossing the former parade ground of the palace, there is an observation point with fine views over the bay.

Leaving the gardens, set high above the city, is the notorious **Detroit Café**, made famous during the 1960s by the Rolling Stones who recorded local musicians while staying with the restaurant owner and beat poet, Brion Gysin. Today, the café is filled with tour groups enjoying the stunning views across the bay and the rooftops of the kasbah.

In the medina's southern corner, hidden in a maze of alleyways, lies a US national monument, the **American Legation★**. This former consulate, donated to President Monroe by Sultan Moulay Suleiman in 1821, now houses a gallery of works by contemporary Moroccan and western artists, and a museum with maps and documents tracing Tangier's history, and the relationship between the US and Morocco.

Beyond the Medina

One of the steep streets leading from Tangier's kasbah to the medina.

Outside the medina, the architecture and feel is colonial. South of the Grand Socco is **Place de France**, home of Tangier's most famous café, the **Café de France**. A few

The Forbes Museum is housed in the Mendoub Palace, former villa of the American millionaire publisher Malcolm Forbes.

doors down is the **El Minzah**, a luxurious hotel which served as headquarters for secret agents during the Second World War and now greets royalty and movie stars.

Tourist development in the town has focused on the sandy bay and the **Avenue des Far**, with its numerous hotels, restaurants and beach clubs. Wealthier visitors have long eschewed the bay in favour of the aptly named wooded district of **La Montagne** (The Mountain) to the west of the port. Its quiet streets and tree-lined squares stand in sharp contrast to the busy commercialism of the medina.

On the outskirts of Tangier along the coast, is the **Musée Forbes★** (Forbes Museum) displaying Malcolm Forbes' huge collection of miniatures of famous battle scenes. There are splendid views from the lovely gardens.

NORTH-WEST COAST

To the west of Tangier lies the dramatic and beautiful spot, **Cap Spartel★**, the north-west tip of Africa where the Atlantic meets the Mediterranean. This is an excellent place to watch migrating birds making the short flight across the Straits of Gibraltar. Look out in particular for wheeling flocks of buzzards, eagles and storks. Across the sea to the north lies Cabo Trafalgar, where Lord Nelson fought his last battle.

Below the Cap, hidden in the rock, are the notorious **Grottes d'Hercule★** (Caves of Hercules). These natural caves have an ancient history: in 1920 French archaeologists discovered relics from a prehistoric cult that worshipped the male phallus. More recently, stonemasons used the caves to cut rocks for millstones, and the marks made by them can still be seen on the cave roofs. The combined effects of sea and man have created spectacular shapes and a series of blow holes.

The unusual natural formations of the Caves of Hercules have been used for centuries to cut millstones.

31

One of the decorative murals to be discovered on the walls of Asilah.

Continuing south along the immense Atlantic coast lies the walled town of **Asilah★**, a popular destination for Moroccan tourists. Its white houses and cobbled streets have a relaxed charm, and its atmosphere is reassuringly laid-back. In August the town hosts an International Arts Festival, attended by top-class bands, singers and artists. Each summer, artists add new works to the colourful and vibrant murals which already decorate many of the medieval Portuguese walls.

Further south, the small town of **Larache** has retained its Spanish ambience. This was the main Spanish port during colonial occupation. Spanish street and shop signs can still be seen, and many locals speak Spanish. Other remnants include the former Spanish cathedral and a ruined 17C fortress, nicknamed **Château de la Cigogne** (Stork Castle), after the national bird which nests there in summer. The local beach is long and sandy and is relatively safe for swimming, compared to beaches further south.

Larache's major claim to fame is its proximity to the Roman ruins of **Lixus★**. Hercules is said to have been sent to Lixus, as his penultimate labour, to steal the golden apples (thought to be tangerines) from the Garden of the Hesperides. In Roman days, the town was the centre for *garum* production, a highly-spiced anchovy paste packed into jars and shipped to Rome. There are several Roman remains to explore, including a few factories, the amphitheatre and a bath house dedicated to Neptune, which has a fine mosaic of the sea-god Oceanus.

THE RIF

The landscape of the Rif mountains is unlike any other in Africa – lofty peaks hidden by cloud, lush green valleys, jagged rocky outcrops, a wild and unpredictable region, once ruled by fierce tribes. The Rif was known to colonial forces as the *Bled es Siba*, the ungovernable land, and it lived up to its name, often acting as a base for quasi-terrorist groups of local tribes during French and Spanish occupation. Its isolation and extreme beauty have recently attracted a new conqueror – the mighty tourist. The area was once the centre of *kif* (hashish) production, but European Union aid has helped wipe out drug plantations and along the coast new resorts are developing, offering the latest in holiday comfort.

Tetouan★★

The main town of the region, Tetouan is a sprawling settlement of white houses. Once capital of Spanish-occupied Morocco, it is still referred to as 'the Daughter of Granada'. The Spanish influence can be seen throughout the town: Art Deco buildings remain amidst the traditional houses, and locals still speak Spanish.

At the heart of the town is a **medina★★** which has several thriving souks and a few museums that are worth a visit. Tetouan produces some of the best craftwork in Morocco, thanks to its famous **Handicrafts School**, built by the Spanish in 1936 and located outside the medina walls at Bab el Okla. Tours can be taken around the classrooms – the school's display room is particularly impressive.

Just inside the medina walls the small **Musée des Arts et Traditions Populaires★** (Folklore Museum), houses older works of art, including a collection of Andalucian Jewish and Islamic embroidery. Hire a guide to take you to **Souk El Hots**, the Berber market specialising in crafts and textiles such as traditional red and white *foutas* (skirts). In Place Moulay-el-Mehdi, the **Musée Archéologique★** (Archaeological Museum) houses relics from Roman Lixus (*see* p.33).

North of Tetouan, along the fine sandy peninsula, lie some of Morocco's newest

The mosque in Chefchaouèn has a distinctive octagonal minaret.

beach resorts. Nearest to Tetouan is **Martil**, a one-time pirate port, now an expanding resort. A new golf course has been built at **Cabo Negro** with villa complexes attached. Further north **Marina Smir** is the most recent resort, complete with yachting marina and the Blue Lagoon Aquaparc.

Chefchaouèn★★ (Chaouen, Chechaouèn, Xauen)
Its dramatic setting beneath the twin peaks of Jbel Chaouen (Chaouen means 'the horns' in Berber) and the delightful maze of white-washed buildings make Chefchaouèn an attractive alternative base to Tetouan.

Its remote setting suited the Muslims and

Andalucian Jews who settled here after escaping the Spanish Inquisition. They lived in splendid isolation until Spanish soldiers captured the town in 1920, to find locals speaking Andalucian dialects that had not been spoken in Spain since the Middle Ages. The red-tiled roofs of the **medina★★** remind one of the 'white villages' of Granada. Today, it's a relaxed and friendly place, and a good base for hiking.

Ketama and Ouazzane

Ketama is the centre of the Rif and traditionally the base of kif production, so visitors are advised to exercise caution (*see* p.113); there is little to see, and most visitors will simply pass through. In contrast, **Ouazzane★** is a quieter town, producing the finest oil in Morocco from 600 000 olive trees. Situated on the gentle slopes of the Djebala mountains, the town is refreshingly uncommercialised and offers an insight into Moroccan rural life. On Thursday mornings the mountain farmers flock to Ouazzane for the atmospheric souk, held in the Place de l'Indépendance. A network of interesting cobbled streets leading off from the square are worth exploring.

NORTHERN COAST

Two geo-political curiosities lie along the north coast: the ports of **Ceuta★** and **Melilla** remained 'Sovereign Territory of Spain' after the Spanish left Morocco in 1956. While neither have any 'sights' to speak of, both have a Spanish ambience worth experiencing and offer duty-free shopping. Ceuta, the biggest, lies at the northernmost tip of Morocco, opposite the British enclave of Gibraltar. Ferries depart regularly for

Spain. Further east is Melilla, a former export port for zinc. Border-crossing formalities into each enclave can be time-consuming, and hire cars are not permitted to cross the border.

Al Hoceima★, some 203km (126 miles) east of Tangier, is one of the largest resorts on the coast, favoured by French and German package-holiday companies, famed for its wide bay and extensive beach, backed by massive cliffs.

Inland, to the south-east, are the **Beni-Snassen Mountains★★**. These green and fertile mountains offer striking scenery and several interesting sites. The **Grotte du Chameau** (Camel's Cave) has large stalactites, one of which resembles a camel and gives the cave its name. The nearby **Gorges du Zegzel★** (Zegzel Gorge) is a dramatic limestone fault cutting between high peaks.

Taking a break between customers on the beach at Tangier.

The Medina

A medina is the old walled quarters of a Moroccan town, the word originating from the city where the Prophet Mohammed settled in 622. Wandering an intricate maze of alleyways, passages and streets can be daunting, but often provides the most memorable moments of a Moroccan holiday. It is advisable to hire a guide to navigate the medina (official guides are certified by the local authorities). The Fès medina is one of the greatest urban experiences in the world – one square mile containing 250 000 inhabitants.

A medina consists of several *derbs* (districts). Each *derb* is a small independent village, containing a mosque, a *hammam* (baths), a bakery, a *medersa* (a koranic school) and a fountain. The *derb* traditionally houses families of all socio-economic levels, a unified community in which rich help poor.

Yet the modern world is encroaching on the ancient medina. As the economy improves, businesses and wealthier families are leaving the cramped conditions for the more spacious suburbs. Buildings are crumbling, shops closing and traditions rapidly disappearing. The hope of UNESCO and the Moroccan government is that money from tourism can be used to preserve the remarkable architecture and culture of the medina.

Right: Rabat medina.
Below: A shoe shop.

CENTRAL PLAINS

The delightful central plains are the most fertile region of Morocco.

The central plains of Morocco are the spiritual, agricultural and political heart of the country. This region, lying between the northern Rif and the central Middle Atlas mountains, is the most fertile in Morocco, producing the bulk of the country's food and much of its exotic fruit and vegetable exports.

To the west is the industrialised Atlantic coast, with urban sprawls stretching between the business centre of Casablanca and the political centre of Rabat, and containing over a third of Morocco's population. In the midst of the plains lies Fès, the first imperial capital and one of the most mysterious and architecturally stunning cities in the world.

Nearby, the omnipotent sultan Moulay Ismaïl constructed one of the world's greatest walled cities as his capital – the monumental metropolis of Meknès.

In the east of the region, the Middle Atlas mountains stretch southwards from Fès, a land of giant cedar forests, Barbary apes and Berber villages.

CASABLANCA★

The popular romantic image of Casablanca is based on scenes from the film *Casablanca*, starring Humphrey Bogart, which was actually shot in Hollywood and bears no resemblance to the city. In reality, Casablanca is much like any other modern city in Europe, with towering office blocks and suburban sprawl.

The modern city of Casablanca, with Place Mohammed V in the foreground.

A striking blue tiled arch, in the Hassan II Mosque.

The city's Phoenician origins are in Anfa, a suburb west of the city, though there may have been prehistoric settlers before this time. There was a Berber settlement when the Arabs arrived in the 7C. During the 13C and 14C pirates used the town as a base from which to launch attacks on Portuguese and Spanish ships. The Portuguese themselves first settled the coast in the 15C and named their port Casa Branca – 'the white house'.

This settlement was destroyed by the Great Earthquake of 1755, and it was not until Arab merchants began to settle in the late 18C that the ruins were cleared and a medina built. Today, the city has a population of more than 3 million, and is a modern bustling business centre, with bold plans to make itself Africa's leading financial centre north of Johannesburg.

Mosquée Hassan II★★★ (Hassan II Mosque)

The main attraction in Casablanca is its vast new mosque, opened in 1993 – a tribute to the vision of King Hassan, and to the generosity of the Moroccan population, for most of the $600 million (£400 million) cost was met by public subscription. It is the second largest mosque in the world, with the world's tallest minaret at 200m (656ft), emitting a laser beam which points to Mecca. The interior prayer hall accommodates 20 000 worshippers with room for a further 80 000 in the exterior courtyard, totalling an astounding 9ha (22 acres). Inspired by the Koran, which says 'the throne of God lies on the water', the mosque's site is as stunning as its architecture, with Atlantic waves crashing up against its white marble walls.

Central Casablanca

The architecture in central Casablanca is colonial French, with the best examples found in the former administrative buildings of **Place Mohammed V★**. To get away from the hectic business centre, walk south from Place Mohammed V to the **Parc de la Ligue Arabe★** (Arab League Garden), with its pleasant cafés, shaded by palm trees. At the north end of the park is the white

Cathédrale du Sacré-Coeur (Sacred Heart Cathedral), the former French cathedral but scheduled to be converted to secular use.

As the French created a city from the dust of the neglected port, thousands of Moroccans flocked from the countryside, looking for work. To house these workers a new medina known as the **Nouvelle Medina★** or **quartier des habous**, was built in the 1930s by French architects in traditional Moroccan style.

Today, the Nouvelle Medina is a thriving market, and a great place to wander, taking in the massive law courts and the mosque. To the east, are the walls of the **Palais du Roi** (Royal Palace), guarded by rather intimidating soldiers.

Âïn-Diab

South of the Hassan II Mosque, the coastal road leads to Âïn-Diab, a strip of cosmopolitan beach clubs, bars and fish restaurants that seems more European than Moroccan. Further on, the long beach of **Sidi-Abd-er-Rahmane** leads to a **marabout** (sacred tomb) on an offshore island, which is cut off at high tide. The shrine is visited by

The beach at Âïn-Diab is lined with pools, bars and clubs.

pilgrims in search of a cure for ailments. Although non-Muslims are not allowed to visit this sacred shrine, it can be viewed from the beach, which is perfect for evening walks, with unforgettable sunsets.

FÈS★★★

There is no other city quite like Fès, the oldest of Morocco's imperial cities. It was founded in the late 8C, the capital of Morocco's first Muslim state. Its old medina is one of the most complete Islamic medieval cities in the world, with a tumultuous maze of streets, craft workshops and mosques that make the senses reel. Thanks to an ambitious renovation programme backed by UNESCO, many of

This broad valley, surrounded by hills, was an ideal setting for the imperial city of Fès.

the city's ancient buildings are being restored to their former glory.

With a population of around 500 000, Fès is divided into three parts: Fès-el-Bali (Old Fès), Fès-Jdid (New Fès) and Ville Nouvelle (the new French-built quarter).

Bab Bou Jeloud, the gateway to Fès.

Fès-el-Bali★★★

Fès-el-Bali is the oldest part of the city, populated in the 9C by Shiite refugees from Tunisia. It is a labyrinth of tiny alleyways, passages and streets in which it is all too easy to get lost or disorientated, so you are advised to take a guided tour. The 16km (10 mile) drive along the **ramparts** provides an excellent introduction to the city.

Bab Bou Jeloud is the grand gateway to Fès, built in 1913 in traditional style, with a central archway flanked by keyhole doorways on either side. The exterior tiles are blue, the colour of Fès, while the green ones on the inside represent Islam.

Fès Medersas

Developed by the Merenids in the 14C, the medersas were ecclesiastical colleges linked to the Karaouiyne University. **Medersa Bou Inania★★**, located just inside the medina from Bab Bou Jeloud, is the only functioning religious building in the city open to non-Muslims, boasting an exquisite central courtyard and prayer hall. The other medersas are no longer used for religious study. **Medersa Attarine★** is not as large as Medersa Bou Inania, but the quality of the stucco work, intricately-carved cedar panels and the lavishly decorated interior make this the most beautiful of all the medersas. **Medersa Cherratine★** is the largest and most recent medersa, built by the Alaouites in 1670. Hidden away down a small lane off Place Seffarine, **Medersa Seffarine** is the oldest college, founded in 1285. Small and unimposing, its interior resembles a traditional house rather than a school. The often-overlooked **Medersa Sahrij**, built in 1321, is noteworthy for the intricate carvings around the walls that are reflected in a small ablutions pool.

Souks

Fès is a great centre for craftsmen of all types, and as you wander round the city you will come across the various souks (markets) devoted to different crafts and goods.

Attarine Souk★ specialises in spices, **Kissaria** is the centre for materials and fabrics, **Chérabliyn Souk** is the place to buy traditional slippers. The highlight of any tour of Fès is the **Souk des Teinturiers** (dyers' souk) – a chaotic warren of blackened workshops where half-naked workers leap between pits of bubbling dyes with youthful grace. The area just below Seffarine is where you will find the tanners who, like the dyers, use the river's water. The scene is unforgettable, as is the smell of the district, emanating from the blend of pigeon droppings used to soften the leather. Beyond the colouring pits, the skins are left to dry for several days on surrounding hills.

In the **Nejjarine Souk** (carpenter's souk) craftsmen saw and hammer cedarwood. At the end of the street is the tranquillity of

These circular vats are used to dye the skins before they are spread out to dry on the hillsides.

Place Nejjarine★★, where you will see the 18C fountain which still provides water for workshops and bakeries in the quarter.

The **Zaouïa de Moulay Idriss★★** (Shrine of Moulay Idriss) is one of the most sacred sites in Morocco, containing the remains of Moulay Idriss II, the founder of Fès. Non-Muslims cannot enter, but can look at the sumptuous interior from the wooden bar that denotes the sanctuary limits (you should not take photographs). Those permitted to enter are said to be blessed by the spirit of the great leader and will enjoy everlasting good fortune.

Once the biggest mosque in North Africa, **Mosquée Karaouiyne★** (Karaouiyne Mosque) remains largely shrouded from view to non-Muslims, although tantalising glimpses are possible from the fourteen gateways (ten of which are open on Fridays). Founded in 859 by Fatima el Fihri, in memory of her Tunisian father, this is the holiest ground in Morocco and site of the greatest university of the ancient Arab world. Added to over the years by different dynasties, the minaret is the oldest remnant, dating from 956. A few religious courses are still held in the mosque's courtyard, and the Islamic library is considered one of the finest in the world.

The best **view** over the medina and the Karaouiyne can be had for the price of a mint tea at the Palais de Fès carpet shop and café, a converted 19C palace.

The **Mosquée des Andalous★** (Andalous Mosque) was built in 860 by Miriam, sister of Fatima who built the Karaouiyne Mosque. It was added to in the 13C by the Almohads, who constructed the gargantuan doorway. The mosque is not open to the public.

Fès-Jdid

Built by the Merenids in 1276, 'Fès the New' was for centuries Morocco's capital until the French created a new administration in Rabat. The 14C **Bab Dekakine (**Gate of the Benches) is an impressively fortified entrance into Fès-Jdid, so-called because this was where criminals were tried, hung and occasionally stuffed as a warning to future miscreants.

The area is dominated by the **Dar el Makhzen** (Royal Palace), the biggest royal palace in Morocco (closed to visitors). The most impressive aspect of the palace is found on **Place des Alaouites**.

Fès was home to thousands of Jewish exiles from the Spanish Inquisition. Their district was known as the **Mellah**, meaning 'salt', alluding to the fact that Jewish inhabitants were given the task of emptying and salting the heads of the Sultan's enemies before they were displayed on the city gates. The Mellah was vacated by most of its original Jewish population of 17 000, who left for Israel following the 1967 Arab-Israeli War. All that remains of their presence is the haunting Hebrew cemetery – the white graves a reminder of a once thriving community.

In the late 19C, Hassan I built the vast **Palais Dar Batha★**, only to die shortly afterwards. The buildings now house a **crafts museum★**, with a fine collection of exhibits apparently randomly displayed, including delicate blue Fès pottery, Berber jewellery, carpets, illustrated Korans, carved cedar, sculptures and stone carvings, guns and coins. Concerts are held here in summer.

Constructed high up on the northern hills of the city, the **Tombeaux Mérenides**

(Merenid Tombs) originally housed the
bodies of Merenid sultans. This point offers
some of the best **views***** of the valley –
from here you can clearly make out the
layout and landmarks of the city and the
seething mass of the medina below. On the
same hillside is the fortress of **Borj Nord**,
built by Sultan El Mansour in the 16C to
guard him from the locals. It, too, offers a
spectacular view over the valley and houses a
military museum.

*The city of Fès, at
dusk, seen from the
hills.*

The ramparts and minaret of the Lalla Aouda Mosque, Meknès, from which only eunuchs were allowed to make the call to prayer.

Meknès★★

Founded in the 10C by the Meknassa Berber tribe, Meknès' glory days came 700 years later when Sultan Moulay Ismaïl decided to build a new capital at Meknès, a city which had remained loyal to him. Leaving the original walled **medina★★** largely as it was, he built his imperial city to the south, using a workforce of 50 000 Berbers and Europeans.

Moulay Ismaïl is part of Moroccan folklore. He defended his lands against foreign invaders ruthlessly, had 500 concubines and countless children, and is said to have put to death 36 000 people with his own hand. To protect him he engaged an army of 25 000 black slaves, whose descendants still act as bodyguards for the king to this day. Yet for all his cruelty and apparently tyrannical rule, Moulay Ismaïl's political achievements and military conquests were impressive (*see* p.12).

Dar Kebira (Imperial City)

Much of the vast **Dar Kebira** (Imperial City) created by Moulay Ismaïl is now in ruins; the Great Earthquake of 1755 shattered the royal palace, and his son and grandson altered much of his city. At its inauguration in 1677, the imperial city contained 50 palaces; now only the walls remain to impress – 25km (12.5miles) of high, sandy battlements, including **The Interminable Wall** or 'Wall of Death', where prisoners marched to their execution. Dominating the central square of the medina, **Place el Hédime**, is **Bab Mansour★★**, the triumphal entrance to the city, named after its architect, Mansour el Aleuj, a Christian slave. The highly-ornamented and richly coloured tiles contrast with the Ionic pillars on either side, which were taken by Moulay Ismaïl from the Roman ruins of Volubilis. Moulay Ismaïl himself is buried alongside the walls. The **Mausoleum★** is open to non-Muslims, but all visitors are required to dress appropriately. The sultan's tomb lies past a series of courtyards in a lavishly-decorated, heavily gilded room.

Further on from the Mausoleum is the **Koubbet el Khiyatin**, a vast chamber used as a reception room for foreign ambassadors and to auction slaves. Next to it is the 'Prison of Christian Slaves', supposedly where the 25 000 Christian slaves Moulay Ismaïl used to build his great city were locked at night.

Other sources say that the slaves were never housed here, and that these subterranean passages were store rooms, but Meknès tour guides prefer the former.

At the **Dar el Ma★**, also known as the Heri as Souani (Royal Granary) is a large, square vaulted building, with a series of elegant arches, which once contained vast grain supplies. The rooms are sometimes described as the royal stables, but are too small to have contained the 12 000 horses Moulay Ismaïl possessed.

Next door to the granaries is Meknès' most refreshing sight – the **Bassin de l'Aguedal** (Aguedal Basin). This huge pool was built to provide water and irrigation during sieges and to entertain the sultan's impressive harem on hot days. Nowadays it is popular for picnicking, bathing and washing cars.

Outside the imperial city are relics of earlier and later eras. The **Medersa Bou Inania★**, probably the finest religious edifice

A pool stands at the centre of the tall, rectangular court of the Medersa Bou Inania.

in Morocco, was built by the architect of the medersas in Fès and adorned with exquisite calligraphy.

The 19C **Dar Jamaï Museum★**, housed in a vizier's palace, has displays of Moroccan arts and crafts, including ceramics and jewellery, and Middle Atlas carpets. The vizier's sumptuous reception room on the upper floor is noteworthy for its ornate ceiling.

Moulay-Idriss★★

The resting place of Moulay Idriss I, direct descendant of the Prophet Mohammed, this town is a major pilgrimage destination for Moroccans. Until 1920, non-Muslims found here would be executed, but today you can wander through the white streets up to the wooden bar that blocks the tomb's entrance.

The town is the site of Morocco's most important and colourful festival, the highly religious (but usually open to non-Muslims) **moussem** of Moulay Idriss, held in August or September.

Volubilis★

The well-preserved Roman town of Volubilis is situated in the fertile plains north of Meknès. Once a Neolithic settlement, the Berbers were established on the site when the Romans arrived in the first century BC. In 25BC Emperor Augustus granted Mauretania to Juba II. Juba, part Berber and part Cartheginian, and reputed to be a descendant of Hannibal, married Cleopatra's daughter. Volubilis is famous for its breathtaking house mosaics scattered throughout the site, excavated by French archaeologists in 1915. Just down from the entrance, the **House of Orpheus** contains a mosaic of the Greek hero and his lyre. In

Mosaic from the Roman ruins of Volubilis.

neighbouring houses other mosaics celebrate Poseidon, Dionysus and Hercules.

The street-plan dating from the 3C town is still visible today. The **Basilica** and **Temple of Jupiter** command the centre, from where the street runs north to an impressive **triumphal arch**. From the arch, the main street, Decumanus Maximus, heads north-east, flanked on each side by the grandest houses, with mosaics in various states of preservation.

RABAT★★★

The political capital since 1912 and European in character, Rabat is a varied cosmopolitan metropolis and offers perhaps the best introduction to the country. Easy to navigate, less frenetic than other Moroccan cities, Rabat still offers some striking imperial monuments.

Rabat's most impressive buildings are found on the shores of the **Bou Regreg** estuary. The **Tour Hassan★★** (Hassan Tower) was designed to be the grandest mosque in the world, a monument to Yacoub El Mansour's victories in Spain. Begun around

Rabat, seen from the Bou Regreg estuary.

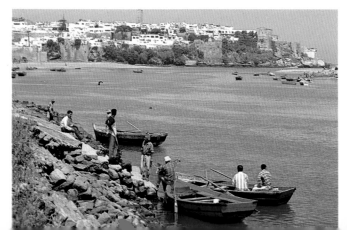

1195, building work stopped when El Mansour died in 1199, leaving the tower as a reminder of what might have been. With different fine stone carvings on each of its sides, the minaret is 44m (145ft) high, and although the immense roof of the mosque was destroyed by the Great Earthquake of 1755, some 312 stunted columns remain as a memorial to imperial extravagance.

To the south of the tower is the **Mausolée de Mohammed V★** (Mausoleum of Mohammed V), the present king's father, who died in 1961. This lavish building, with its distinctive green-tiled pyramidal roof topped with three golden spheres, was designed by Vietnamese architect Vo Toan. Inside, the tomb is a stunning work of art, with polished marble, onyx, brasswork, stucco and cedar carving.

At the mouth of the Salé estuary is the 12C **Kasbah des Oudaïas★★**, built by the Almohads. You enter by grandiose **Bab Oudaïa★★**, which impresses not by its sheer size or elaborate decoration, but by the sense of balance and unity in its form. Rue Jemaa leads to a sweeping terrace, with **views** out to the Atlantic. In one corner of the square is a small **carpet workshop** where women demonstrate weaving techniques.

The Merenids eschewed Almohad architecture in favour of their own. The **Chellah★★** contains some of the most evocative ruins in Morocco, set in a tropical garden populated by white storks. Here are the remains of ancient Roman Sala Colonia and the tomb of the mighty Merenid leader, El Hassan, the 'Black Sultan'. It is a magical site – a pool by the tombs is said to grant fertility if you feed a boiled egg to the eels that live there.

Museums

As befits a capital city, Rabat contains a number of fine museums. Inside the kasbah, Moulay Ismaïl's former palace now houses the excellent **Musée des Arts Marocains★** (Moroccan Crafts Museum), with displays of pottery, costumes, musical instruments, armour, jewellery and a representation of Fassi and R'bati wedding ceremonies. After your visit have a drink at the café in the surrounding Andalusian gardens, which are among the loveliest in Morocco.

In town, the excellent **Musée Archéologique★** (Archaeological Museum) houses impressive relics from Volubilis, including a unique collection of bronze statues, notably the nearly 2 000-year-old busts of Juba II and Cato. There are important finds from the Roman city of Sala Colonia, and artefacts from Taforalt, and the Neolithic sites at Skhirate and Harhoura.

Shopping is a delight in Rabat. The **medina** is bustling and friendly. Rabati carpets are perhaps the best in Morocco; **Rue des Consuls★** is lined with carpet shops. The covered **Souk es Sabet** specialises in gold-stamped leatherwork, and there are a number of nearby specialist souks where crafts can be bought.

Across the estuary, **Salé★★** was one of the most feared pirate bases in Africa. Behind the medina is the **Grande Mosquée** (Great Mosque) and **medersa★**, built by El Hassan in 1341. Although non-Muslims may not enter the mosque, they are allowed to visit the medersa. A climb to the roof will be rewarded with **views** across the estuary to Rabat.

South of Rabat

Extending south along the **Atlantic coast** are

a series of long sandy beaches and small resorts. The most fashionable beaches are south of Rabat: **Temara** and **Skhirat-Plage** (home to King Hassan's summer palace) are the haunts of the most chic holidaymakers. The Atlantic currents are very strong along this coast, so care is needed when swimming.

Further south is the majestic Portuguese port of **El-Jadida★★** and its sandy medina. Down some steps is the spectacular 16C **Portuguese Cistern★★**, now containing just a few inches of water, making this a most attractive water tank as the rays of light from the central skylight create a magical pattern in the vaulted room. It was used in Orson Welles' film *Othello* in 1949. You can also climb the wide Portuguese battlements high above the medina and the Atlantic.

One of the finest beaches along this coast is found outside **Azemmour**, a small white fishing port perched on the banks of the **Oum er-Rbia**. From the windswept ramparts you can see as far as Casablanca on a clear day.

The vaulted ceilings reflect in the water as the light streams into the Portuguese Cistern in El-Jadida.

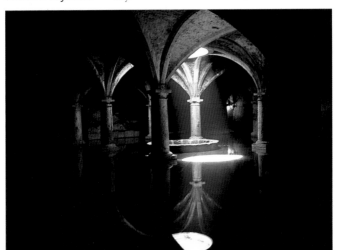

MIDDLE ATLAS (MOYEN ATLAS)

The Middle Atlas are a series of mountains 60km (37 miles) south of Fès, a region of cedar-clad slopes, rocky outcrops leading to the vast limestone plateaux, and cool lakes. The centre of the region is **Beni-Mellal★**, a fast-growing modern city with a population of 200 000, fringed with orange and olive trees. The finest drives in the region run south of Fès along the **Sefrou★** and **Ifrane★ valleys**. The Ifrane valley is the most attractive, rising to the town of **Imouzzèr-du-Kandar** from where dirt tracks continue east to a series of small lakes. Further south is Ifrane, created by the French in 1929 as a retreat for city dwellers during the hot summers, offering cool, fragrant mountain breezes. It is also a winter ski centre serving

The mountain resort of Ifrane has a distinctive Alpine ambience.

nearby **Mischliffen★**, which has basic ski facilities.

The road from Ifrane to Azrou offers impressive views of the mountain ranges, descending to the plateau. **Azrou★** is a quiet town, built on a wooded hillside next to the rocky outcrop which gives the town its name (*azrou* = rock). It is famous for its wood crafts, displayed in the **Maison de l'Artisanat** (Craftsmanship House).

The Sefrou valley is more sparsely populated, with few towns, but you should not miss the ancient walled town of **Sefrou★** itself. Set in the heart of the **cedar forest★★** is **Aïn-Leuh**, where you may encounter groups of **Barbary apes**. But be warned: they do not like being approached, and think nothing of launching missiles at anyone who comes too close.

Barbary apes.

Going south on the P 24, after about 35km (23 miles) you will find, among many streams and springs, the headwaters of one of the country's important rivers, the Oum-er-Rbia. **Midelt**, below the **Jbel Ayachi** mountains, is a town renowned for its carpet manufacture and is a convenient stopping-off point. Adventurous drivers will want to head west on route 3424 to the **Cirque de Jaffar★**, a rough track that climbs to 3 700m (12 870ft), with spectacular views as the reward for the precarious drive.

The only natural pass between the Middle Atlas and the Eastern Rif is the **Taza Gap**. As befits its strategic position, **Taza★** is a highly fortified town – the 12C Almohad ramparts extend 3km (1.8 miles). It is relatively unaffected by tourism, and has an intriguing **Berber Souk** in the **medina★**. Taza is gateway to the forested highlands of **Jbel Tazzeka National Park**, popular with hikers.

MARRAKECH AND THE HIGH ATLAS (HAUT ATLAS)

Marrakech is the cultural heart of the country, a city full of passion and energy. The most popular tourist destination in Morocco, it remains a most intriguing city, a place of magnificent architecture, vast palm oases and magical souks.

To the west of the city is the Atlantic coast and the pretty port of Essaouira; behind it soar the High Atlas mountains, named after the mythological giant who was condemned by Zeus to hold up the sky at the edge of the world. This mountainous region is unlike any other in Morocco: remote and isolated, often cut off by winter snow, the small Berber villages are inhabited largely by sheep farmers making a meagre living in often harsh conditions. Untouched by tourism, they are some of the most open and friendly people in the country.

MARRAKECH★★★

The city was built by the Almoravid Berbers in the 11C as a base for their rampaging conquests into Europe and Eastern Africa. Today, it is still the gateway to the immense continent to the south.

The heart of Marrakech is the **Jemaa el Fna★★★**, a huge square that remains one of the world's last great informal circuses. Acrobats and musicians leap and dance, monkeys scamper, and snake-charmers, jugglers, storytellers and scribes all compete for attention. The best hour to be there is around sunset, when the square becomes an open-air restaurant, itinerant food stalls providing such delicacies as goat's head soup, grilled or fried vegetables, chicken, fish and mutton.

The Jemaa el Fna by day is calm compared with the frenetic atmosphere that permeates the square after sunset.

The name Jemaa el Fna means 'assembly of the dead' because, some claim, this was the place where criminals were executed in the 13C. For the best view over the colourful chaos, find a table on the terrace of **Café de la Place** or **Café Glacier**.

South of the square is the symbol of Marrakech, the **Koutoubia Minaret★★★**, built by the Almohads in 1158. The Koutoubia takes it name from the 12C booksellers and binders – the *kutubiyyin* – who gathered at its base. The elegant tower is the basic model

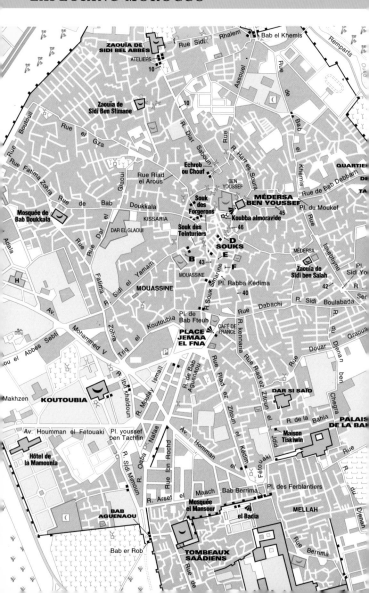

At 70m (230ft) the Koutoubia Minaret is the tallest landmark in Marrakech.

for all Moroccan minarets, copied in numerous towers around the country, including the new Hassan II Mosque, in Casablanca.

The Medina★★★ and its Souks★★

The medina of Marrakech is a colourful, chaotic maze of streets and courtyards, linking areas trading in the traditional arts and crafts of Morocco, though with a more exotic flavour than the souks of Fès. The crafts have an African flavour, whilst the **Rhaba Kédima** (apothecaries' souk) offers dried lizards, porcupines, snakes and hedgehogs – delicacies from which you can concoct your own love potion or charm.

On the fringes of the souks are more

Map of Marrakech.

You can buy almost anything – from a love potion to a pair of shoes – in the souks of Marrakech.

sedate religious buildings. The **Medersa** and **Mosquée ben Youssef**★★ were begun by the Merenids in the 14C and replaced by the Saadians in the 16C. The college was the largest in Morocco, housing 900 students; the building seems immense compared to the claustrophobic colleges of Fès. Nearby stands the **Koubba Ba'Adiyn**, the sole Almoravid monument in the city, dating from the 12C. The small domed shrine is stunning in its simplicity, with its scalloped and horseshoe arches, crenallated battlements and reliefs. It represents characteristic architectural shapes and forms which are mirrored throughout Morocco.

Palaces

Marrakech is a city of palaces. The oldest is the **Palais El Badia** (El Badia Palace), built by El Mansour. It was the most splendid palace in Africa at its completion in 1603, adorned with finest marble from Italy. When Sultan El Mansour asked his court jester what he thought of the palace, hoping for compliments, the jester replied that it would make a fine ruin; within 100 days, the sultan had died and Moulay Ismaïl stripped the

All that remains of the once sumptuous El Badia Palace are the ruined walls, yet its sheer scale is still impressive.

The Saadian Tombs are the resting place of El Mansour and numerous members of his family.

palace of all its finery to embellish Meknès. Little remains, save the huge red walls. It is here that that the world-famous National Folklore Festival is held each June.

El Mansour is buried in the **Tombeaux Saadiens★★★** (Saadian Tombs) next to the palace. Moulay Ismaïl, who destroyed the El Badia, dared not also raze the tombs lest he anger El Mansour's spirit, so instead he sealed them up behind huge walls. It took an aerial survey by the French army in 1917 to reveal their existence, and a corridor was built to allow public access. To avoid the crowds at one of Morocco's most visited sites, get there early in the morning or late afternoon.

Round the corner from El Badia is the **Palais de la Bahia★★** (la Bahia Palace) which became the French governor's residence during colonial days. Built in 1894, la Bahia means 'the brilliant'. Although only a third of the original palace is left, elegantly crumbling, you can take a tour of the luxurious apartments, through the courtyard to the lovely Andalucian gardens.

Marrakech's one museum of note is the **Musée des Arts Marocains★** (Museum of Moroccan Arts and Crafts), located in the former palace of Si Saïd, the brother of the vizier who built the El Bahia. Its collections include carved cedar, copper, pottery, comprehensive displays of Atlas carpets and Berber jewellery.

Gardens and Ramparts★

The people of Marrakech enjoy some of the most beautiful gardens in the world. Of these, perhaps the most seductive is the **Jardin Majorelle★** (Majorelle Garden), a tropical Eden created by French artist

Jacques Majorelle, who lived here from 1922 to 1962. The gardens were bought in 1978 by French fashion designer Yves Saint-Laurent.

The city's largest gardens are the **Jardin de la Ménara** (Ménara Gardens), designed around a huge central pool, fed by channels from the High Atlas. The small Menzeh pavilion was built by Sultan Sidi Mohammed, providing a spectacular image against the palm trees and sweep of the immense Toubkal mountain range. Less immaculate, but more tranquil, are the **Jardin de l'Aguedal★** (Aguedal Gardens) comprising 3km (1.8 miles) of orange, fig, lemon and olive groves. The heart of the gardens is the pool of **Sahraj el Hana**, the 'pool of health' – an ironic name

The Majorelle Gardens offer a tropical paradise in the heart of Marrakech.

considering Sultan Sidi Mohammed
drowned here in 1873.

The gardens of the famous **Mamounia
Hotel** can be enjoyed while sipping a
refreshing mint tea. The Mamounia Palace
was converted into a hotel in the 1920s, and
was used as a location for the 1956 version of
Alfred Hitchcock's *The Man Who Knew Too
Much*. Its fragrant lanes and flower beds are
immaculately maintained, as befits a
sanctuary enjoyed in the past by such guests
as Winston Churchill, Ronald Reagan and
Prince Charles.

A one-time desert fortress, Marrakech
boasts an impressive array of 12C **ramparts★**,
stretching 19km (11.8 miles) around the
city. You can tour the red walls by horse and
carriage, or walk along sections, stopping at
some of the highlights, such as the souk at
Bab El Khemis and the tanneries at **Bab
Debbarh**. To the west, **Bab Doukkala** now
contains a modern art gallery.

ESSAOUIRA★★

There is evidence that this part of the
coastline was known to the Phoenicians and
the Romans, but it was the Portuguese who
established the military and commercial
port of Mogador here at the end of the 15C.
In 1765, the French architect Théodore
Cornut was hired to design the city; the
unique French urban plan can still be seen.
It was at this time that it became known as
Essaouira, meaning 'well-designed'.

It is a most attractive place, with its
characteristic whitewashed buildings with
blue shutters and doors. The port teems
with small fishing boats, while the long
sandy beaches attract windsurfers from
around the world. There are few sights, but

this enchanting town is best enjoyed by simply wandering through the streets, especially the **souks**★, where dark, knotted thuya wood is crafted. You can walk along the **Skala ramparts**★, with views over the islands and the beach, but the most animated place is the **fishing port**★ where trawlers come and go, unloading their catch to a chorus of seagulls. Small seafood grills allow you to sample seafood cooked fresh from the boats.

Some 10km (6.2 miles) south of the port is the magnificent beach and sand dunes of **Diabat** (note that the last 4km/2.5 miles of the access is along a dirt track). As you walk along the beach towards an old ruined fort, the beach becomes cleaner and less busy.

Boat-building in the fishing port of Essaouira.

HIGH ATLAS (HAUT ATLAS)

Soaring mountains, dramatic valleys and tumbling mountain streams are characteristic of the High Atlas region. This is the Ourika Valley, east of Jbel Toubkal.

The High Atlas region is isolated from the rest of Morocco, with huge peaks soaring above the clouds and tiny Berber villages clinging precariously to the mountain sides. Tourism is a new concept in the region, and care must be taken to preserve the ecology and traditions of this lofty land.

In the midst of the High Atlas, and within the **Toubkal National Park**, stands the third highest mountain in Africa, **Jbel Toubkal★★** (Mount Toubkal). Although the ascent takes two days, it is a mountain hike suitable for the fit, rather than a mountain climb for expert climbers only.

East of Jbel Toubkal, the narrow **Ourika Valley★** carves a path through the High Atlas. Productive terraces are cut into the valley sides, watered by melted snow from the mountains. A popular excursion from the summer heat of Marrakech is to drive along the cool, fertile valley to the mountain village of **Setti-Fatma**; the last kilometre is little more than a gravel

track. The path leads on past the houses up to a series of seven waterfalls plunging into deep pools.

An alternative trip from Marrakech is to **Oukaïmeden★★**, branching right off the S 513. The spectacular route twists and climbs through deep canyons beside the stream, past hillside Berber villages. Oukaïmeden is an excellent winter ski resort, and a base for hiking in summer. The prehistoric **rock carvings** are worth a visit.

Tizi-n-Test★★ and Tizi-n-Tichka★★ Passes

There are two routes south through the High Atlas from Marrakech. The **Tizi-n-Test** pass lies south-west of Marrakech. The road ascends from **Asni** to **Ouirgane** and the upper Nfiss valley. Here, above the Nfiss river, dwarfed by soaring mountain peaks, is the mystical ruined **Mosquée de Tinmel★** (Tinmel Mosque). Built in 1153 by the fundamentalist Almohad dynasty as a shrine to their founder, Ibn Toumert, the mosque was also a fortress when besieged by the Merenids in 1276. They destroyed the Almohad town but left the mosque, fearing the spirit of Ibn Toumert. The mosque is still used, despite its ruined walls and lack of roof. The steep road winds some 30km (18.5 miles) up to the Tizi-n-Test pass. From here there are breathtaking views, unfortunately often obscured by mists.

The equally spectacular **Tizi-n-Tichka** pass runs south-east from Marrakech, soaring to 2 260m (7 232ft) at its highest point. The road winds up through forests to the barren summits of the pass and is a memorable journey indeed, descending on the other side to Ouarzazate.

Mountain Life: The Berbers

The Berbers of North Africa are a mysterious people, thought to have originated in ancient Libya. Morocco has the largest percentage of Berbers in North Africa, comprising 60 per cent of its inhabitants. There are more than a thousand different Berber dialects spoken in Morocco, variations of the three main Berber dialects. Almost half Morocco's Berbers do not speak Arabic as their first language. Indeed, in some remote areas little French or even Arabic is understood.

The most traditional Berber tribes are found in the High Atlas. Their isolation is extreme – they have not been ruled by outside powers in over 1000 years and still lead an existence on the fringes of the Moroccan state, receiving no benefits and paying no taxes.

Left inset: Berber tribesman.
Left: Tribesman heading into the mountains, near Imilchil.
Right: Young Berber.

The family is the cornerstone of Berber life. Each household or tent has its own autonomous power structure, but in times of harvest or conflict, families form allegiances to help the village as a whole. They have traditionally been employed in farming and trading, and this is still the case today.

Berber peoples were converts to Islam as early as the 8C, but the Atlas Berbers have also preserved more ancient beliefs – look out for the strange geometric designs on village walls, the magic eye that wards off evil spirits. Ancient tribal laws still hold more sway than Islamic edicts.

But even the remotest High Atlas villages are gradually changing: tents are replaced with makeshift buildings, children attend school, the young leave for the city. An ancient way of life is rapidly vanishing. The hope is that controlled tourism may help to preserve Morocco's Berber traditions.

The endless stretch of sand at Agadir attracts sun-worshippers.

THE SOUTH

In the south of Morocco you will find the desert landscape of your dreams – lush, green palm oases, endless huge sand dunes and camel trains led by men in blue robes. Most visitors stay in the resort of **Agadir**, but the most rewarding sights are found in the inland villages and oases.

AGADIR★

Agadir is Morocco's premier tourist resort, welcoming hundreds of thousands of sunseekers each year. Agadir has little to offer in the way of historic attractions, but it provides a good base for exploring the area. There is little to do here, other than lie on the immense beaches and dance the night away in one of the countless discos. The energetic can indulge in the varied water-sports, or take a camel ride along the sands.

Agadir was completely rebuilt after the town was destroyed just before midnight on the 29 February 1960, when 15 000 people were killed in a huge earthquake. The destroyed city and its dead were buried in a huge mound, to prevent the spread of cholera, and a new city was built to the south.

The ancient **kasbah★** is the only remaining part of the old town, set above the port, providing a fine view north to the mountains and south over the town, a steep but rewarding climb. Along **Rue de la Corniche** you pass the burial mound of **Ancien Talborj**, marking the place where thousands of bodies were buried. The magnificent beach is one of the safest on the Atlantic Coast, though even here there is an under-tow. Café-bars serve one end of the beach, and hotels are fast developing along it.

Above: Agard-Oudad village nestles below Napoleon's Hat.
Right: The painted rocks of Jean Verame.

TAFRAOUTE★★★

(145km/90 miles south-east of Agadir)

In the heart of the Anti-Atlas mountains, the region around Tafraoute is famed for its fantastic rock formations and small colourful villages clinging to the cliffs. The striking contrast between the lush oases and the bare mountain slopes as you drive up to the town of Tafraoute makes this one of the most beautiful trips in the country. The town itself is small, set by a large oasis – a convenient base to explore the area, with its numerous little villages. The S 509 road leads north of the village, providing spectacular views back into the Ameln valley, especially in February when the almond trees are in bloom.

South of Tafraoute is **Agard-Oudad★** sitting at the base of an enormous pyramid of rock that locals nickname 'Napoleon's Hat'. About 10km (6 miles) further on are the extraordinary boulders painted red and blue by the Belgian 'land artist' **Jean Verame**, in the 1980s.

TAROUDANNT★
(80km/50 miles east of Agadir)

A characteristic town of the south, Taroudannt is famous for its battlemented **ramparts★**, built by the Saadians in the 16C and representing some of the best preserved walls in Morocco. They are prettily offset by the orange and olive groves which grow around their base. Horse-drawn carriages offer 5km (3 mile) tours of the ramparts, or you can walk along them. The **souks** are lively and filled with fine local crafts, including Berber silver jewellery and the limestone carvings of the Taroudannt sculptors. For extreme luxury, head south of the town to the **Gazelle d'Or**, possibly the most exclusive hotel in Morocco, set amidst the orange and olive groves.

Taliouine (200km/124 miles east of Agadir) and **Tazenakht** (285km/177 miles east of Agadir) are convenient overnight stopping places between Agadir and Ouarzazate. Taliouine (known for its saffron) is a good base for hiking. At Tazenakht you can buy carpets woven by the Ouzguita tribe.

The frontier town of Taroudannt was defended by these formidable battlements.

DADÈS★ AND TODRA GORGES★★

Âït-Benhaddou★★
(32km/20 miles north of Ouarzazate)

The desert kasbah of Âït-Benhaddou is probably one of the most visited, most photographed and most filmed villages in Morocco. It is quite easy to see why it is so popular; its jumbled mosaic of kasbahs, deep red decorated walls and crenellated towers, set in an arid and barren plain, look like something from a film set. Indeed, it is easy to be deceived, for the main gateway is not old, but was actually built by a film company. Yet the village is a welcoming place – locals invite you into their homes, displaying handicrafts or brewing tea. While farming still continues in the parched valley, tourism is now the village's main source of income.

The red walls of Âït-Benhaddou cover the bare hillside above the barren valley floor.

Situated along the 'Route des Kasbahs'★★ from the oasis of **Skoura**★★ to **Tinerhir**★★ are two gorges of exceptional beauty. East of **El-Kelâa-des-Mgouna**★, a town famed for its rose plantations, the **Dadès Gorge**★ is a dramatic fissure in the rock, cut by the Dadès river. The potholed road along the gorge is accessible by car as far as Msemrir, but four-wheel-drive vehicles may be able to proceed much further. The river valley sides and the broad valley floor further downstream are covered with a pattern of small, family-owned kasbahs; it is known as 'the valley of a thousand kasbahs'. After **Aït-Oudinar** a bridge leads to the gorges.

Further east, the **Todra Gorge**★★ is smaller in scale, but no less breathtaking. Route 6902 leads north through the oasis of Tinerhir, a former French Foreign Legion garrison overlooking magnificent thick palm groves. The ruined Glaoui kasbah dominates the town to the west. In the canyon itself, 300m- (960ft-) high cliffs plunge dramatically to the riverbed. The road continues to a couple of small hotel-restaurants – a magical place to spend a night.

DRÂA VALLEY★★

One of the most spectacular drives in Morocco is south to the fringes of the Sahara desert. The **Drâa river** begins in the High Atlas and vanishes into the sand of the Sahara. Along its course, the valley is a sumptuous sight, laced with palm oases and *ksour* – fortified towns constructed from baked mud. The contrast of this rich, fertile valley with the bare rocks of the mountain sides is a powerful sight. The fertile land is fully utilized, with terraces and irrigation systems, supporting a population of 800 000.

The broad valley of the Dadès is peppered with numerous kasbahs, hence its name 'valley of a thousand kasbahs'.

The gateway to the valley is the dusty town of **Ouarzazate**, a place to stock up before the drive into the desert. The **Glaoui Taourirt kasbah**★★ is still partly inhabited, but several rooms can be explored.

From Ouarzazate the road passes through scorched plains, then climbs over the Jbel Sarhro range to **Agdz**, a village famous for brightly coloured carpets. The most impressive *ksour* in the Drâa are on the east of the road at **Tamnougalt**. Here the oases begin, palm groves laden with dates – as exotic a landscape as anywhere in the world.

Although it at first appears rather dusty and uninviting, **Zagora** has a good range of hotels and is a good base to spend the night. If time allows, pause here to explore the remains of an earlier Almoravid city. Further south, modern facilities disappear and the desert dominates. South of Zagora lies **Tamegroute★**, home to a medersa with one of the few Islamic libraries open to non-Muslims, containing an 11C copy of the Koran. The town is also a centre for pottery, which can be bought at the souk.

Stop at **Tinfou** to see its dramatic 20m (64ft) sand dune, best appreciated at dawn

A trip to the great sweeping sand dunes of the south will fulfill even the most romantic visitor's dreams of the desert.

or dusk. The end of the road is at **Mhamid**, an isolated settlement that once was an important market for nomadic tribes, and a key oasis on the Sahara trade route. From here, you can explore the palm groves and *ksour* of Mhamid, and contemplate the vast, empty expanse of desert ahead of you.

ZIZ VALLEY★ and TAFILALT OASIS★★

The dramatic group of oases of the **Ziz Valley★** extending south from the eastern extremity of the High Atlas range, is the homeland of the Alaouite dynasty. **Er-Rachidia**, the capital of the region, provides a good base for touring the impressive **Ziz Gorge★★** to the north and the awesome oases and desert expanses to the south. On the road to Erfoud, make a detour near **Meski** (23km/14 miles south of Er-Rachidia) to the refreshing **Source Bleue★** – a natural spring which feeds a swimming pool built by the French Foreign Legion. The sleepy town of **Erfoud** is the departure point for visiting some of Morocco's most dramatic landscapes: the **Tafilalt oasis★★** renowned for its one million palms and the red sand dunes of **Erg Chebbi★★** near Merzouga to the east (the road is uncertain and often blocked by sand drifts, but the 150m/480ft dunes are worth the adventure).

In the midst of Tafilalt once stood Morocco's leading Arab and later Islamic City, Sijilmassa – a jewelled metropolis fed by Saharan camel caravans. It was destroyed in the 19C and replaced with the modern **Rissani**, which has a lively souk. A few kilometres south-east of Rissani is the **mausoleum★** of the first Alaouite ruler, Moulay Ali Chérif.

FIGUIG★★
(375km/233 miles south of Oujda)

The most easterly city in Morocco, right on the border with Algeria, Figuig is one of the most dramatic oases in North Africa. Over 200 000 palm trees sit snugly in a valley surrounded by a necklace of jagged mountains. Despite improved accessibility, the lack of hotels and extreme distance from major tourist centres has allowed the town to retain an isolated, relaxed atmosphere, unblemished by tourism and its trappings.

South of the centre, the road ascends to a viewpoint over the seven fortified villages that make up the oasis. The prettiest is **Ksar d'El-Oudarhir★**, with its narrow streets and hot springs.

THE WESTERN SAHARA

Guelmim, 200km (125 miles) south of Agadir, was the final stop on the Saharan camel train route from Ghana to the Atlantic coast. This town is a desert administration post, famous for its camel market each Saturday populated by Morocco's 'blue men', so-called because of their blue robes, dyed with indigo, which stained the skin blue. The market is now staged almost entirely for the benefit of the huge numbers of tourists who are bussed into the town; the camels are sold for meat, rather than as caravan transport animals; and the blue men are more likely to be locals dressed up in blue for the day. However, it makes a colourful and interesting spectacle. During the rest of the week, Guelmim assumes a more relaxed, gentle atmosphere.

The Western Sahara was long a war zone

where Moroccan and Algerian-backed Polisario rebels fought for territory, until peace accords were signed in 1989. Now the region is gradually opening up to tourism, but despite these efforts the presence of the UN is still noticeable. **Laâyoune** is the main city of the region, with a couple of up-market hotels (though often block-booked for UN personnel) offering desert excursions, excellent sea fishing and deserted Atlantic beaches. It was here that King Hassan marched with 250 000 subjects to claim the region for Morocco during the 1975 Green March.

Guelmim market, on the edge of the desert, where the 'blue men' come to trade, is also popular with tourists.

WEATHER

Morocco has long been known as 'a cold country with a hot sun'. The contrast in climates may come as a surprise, but temperatures in the High Atlas can fall as low as -10°C (14°F) in the winter, while summers in the western Sahara regularly top 50°C (122°F). There is often flooding in the Rif mountains, yet some settlements in the pre-Sahara have not seen rain in over ten years.

The best time of year to visit Morocco is in spring or autumn, when there is less likelihood of rain, but the temperature is still comfortable. However, when you go will in part depend on which part of the country you are visiting. In the northern half of the country the winters are wet and mild along the coast, while in the moutains temperatures fall below freezing. Summers in the north are hot and very dry. In the

Sunset over Tafraoute.

deserts of the south it is hot all year, with temperatures reaching a peak of 45°C (112°F), and the rainfall is low, with less (or none at all) falling in the summer.

ACCOMMODATION

There is no shortage of places to stay in Morocco, with the choice ranging from international luxury hotels to mountaintop refuges where hikers can spend the night. At the top end of the market are hotels graded from one to five stars, with prices regulated by the Ministry of Tourism, but unless you are happy with rudimentary facilities, it is probably best to stick to 3-star establishments and above, which are more on a par with European and North American standards.

Approximate price bands, per room per night, are as follows:

    5-star: 600–2 300dh
    4-star: 350–700dh
    3-star: 250–400dh
    2-star: 150–300dh
    1-star: 70–200dh

Unclassified hotels, usually in the medina, are cheaper still but offer limited security and often few modern facilities. Families wanting reasonable accommodation along the coast should choose an apartment on one of the complexes available in the resorts. For young people (aged 13-30), youth hostels or rest centres for young tourists are an option. The Royal Federation of Moroccan Youth Hostels is affiliated to the International Federation of Youth Hostels.

A list of hotels, youth hostels, refuges and rest centres is available from the Moroccan National Tourist Office (*see* p.125).

Accommodation Recommendations
Fès

Hotel Palais Jamaï (*Bab El Ghuissa* ☎ *05-634331*) A famous hotel in the one-time 19C palace of the vizier to Sultan Moulay Hassan. Lovely Andalusian gardens, large heated pool, hammam and enviable position just inside the medina walls, but very expensive.

Jnan Palace (*Ave Ahmed Chaouki* ☎ *05-652230*) A new luxury hotel built in the palace-hotel tradition.

Batha Hotel (*Rue de l'Unesco* ☎ *05-636437*) and **Hotel Moussafir** (*Ave des Almohades* ☎ *05-651902*) Both newer hotels with good facilities and moderate prices.

Grand Hotel (*Blvd Abdallah Chefchaouni* ☎ *05-625511*) An inexpensive, large colonial-style hotel overlooking the gardens of Place Mohammed V.

Marrakech

Mamounia (*Ave Bab Jdid* ☎ *04-448981*) One of the world's top hotels. This former Alaouite palace has hosted many famous people, from Winston Churchill to Ronald Reagan.

Palmeraie Golf Palace (*Ave de France* ☎ *04-448222*) A luxury hotel, complete with 18-hole golf course.

Hotel Imilchil (*Ave Echouhada* ☎ *04-447653*) This inexpensive hotel enjoys a good position close to the medina, with pool, gardens and air conditioning.

Taroudannt

La Gazelle d'Or (*Route de Amezgou* ☎ *08-852039*) Considered Morocco's most luxurious hotel.

Hotel Palais Salam (*Route de Ouarzazate* ☎ *08-852312*) This famous palace was actually constructed as part of the town's medieval walls (expensive).

Hotel Palais Salam,
Taroudannt.

Casablanca
Royal Mansour (*27 Ave des Far* ☎ *02-313011*)
The landmark hotel in Casablanca, built in
the 1950s but with all modern facilities.
Majestic (*55 Blvd Lalla Yacout* ☎ *02-446285*)
A comfortable hotel with atmosphere, good
facilities, moderately priced.
Hotel du Palais (*68 Rue Farhat Hachad*
☎ *02-276191*) A popular inexpensive hotel
in central Casablanca, with spacious rooms.
Meknès
Hotel Rif (*Zankat Accra* ☎ *05-522591*)
A welcoming hotel that has changed little
since the 1960s, with good facilities and a
swimming pool.

Tangier

Hotel El Minzah (*85 Rue de la Liberté* ☎ *09-935885*) One of Morocco's great hotels, and centre of intrigue during the 1920s. Much frequented by movie-stars and politicians.

Continental (*36 Rue Dar el Baroud* ☎ *09-931024*) A characterful 19C establishment, by the medina with harbour views from the terrace. It was used in the film of Paul Bowles' *The Sheltering Sky*.

Chefchaouen

Casa Hassan (*22 Rue Targui* ☎ *09-986153*) Inexpensive bed and breakfast in a converted palace.

Rabat

Hotel Terminus (*384 Ave Mohammed V* ☎ *07-700616*) Well situated and offering good facilities in the middle price range.

Hotel Tour Hassan (*26 Ave Abderrahman Annegai* ☎ *07-726307*) Well appointed (expensive).

Essaouira

Villa Maroc (*10 Rue Abdallah Ben Yassin* ☎ *04-473147*) An exquisite small hotel, just inside the city walls.

Small hotel-restaurant in the Dadès Gorge.

CALENDAR OF EVENTS

Morocco's many *moussems* (religious festivals) are an excellent way to see traditional costumes, dance and music. Most towns and many small villages hold these festivals in honour of a local saint, usually in August or September, after the harvest.

The *fantasia* can form part of a *moussem*, or any other festival, and is an exciting event to watch. Horsemen clothed in full battledress, complete with rifles, charge the crowd, stopping just in time to avoid disaster. After loud war cries and a volley of shots, they retreat just as rapidly in a cloud of dust and thunder of hooves.

Check locally to see what events are on. Below are some of the main festivals, but there are many smaller but equally fascinating ones.

January: International Marathon, Marrakech.

February: Almond Blossom Festival, Tafraoute; National Cuisine Festival, Agadir.

March: Theatre Festival, Casablanca; Cotton Festival, Beni-Mellal.

May: Rose Petal Festival, El-Kelaâ Mgouna, Dadès valley.

June: National Folklore Festival, El Badi Palace, Marrakech; Festival of Cherries, Sefrou; Moussem, Asni, near Marrakech; Saharan Moussem at Tan-Tan; Moussem of Sidi M'Hamed Benamar, including a Camel Festival, near Guelmim; Moussem of Sidi Moussa, Casablanca.

July: Moussem of Outa Hammou, Chaoun; Honey Festival, Imouzzèr-des-Ida-Outanane; Water Festival, Martil near Tetouan.

August: International Arts Festival, Asilah; Moussem of Setti Fatma, Ourika, near

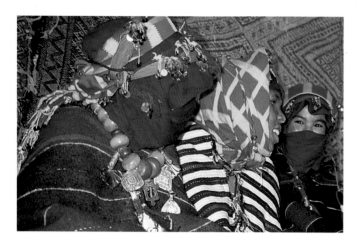

Veiled brides adorned in traditional finery for the Marriage Festival, Imilchil.

Marrakech; Moussem of Dar Zhirou, Rabat; Moussem of Sidi Allal Al Hadh, Chefchaouen; Moussem of Moulay Abdellah, including *fantasia*, near El-Jadida; Festival of African Music, Tiznit; Acrobats Festival, Sidi Ahmed ou Moussa.

September: National *Fantasia* Festival, Meknès, one of the biggest festivals in Morocco; Traditional Arts Festival, Fès; Moussem of Moulay Idriss II, Fès; Moussem of Sidi Ahmed Ou Moussa, Agadir; Marriage Festival, Imilchil; Moussem of Moulay Idriss I, Moulay-Idriss; Festival of African Music, Agadir.

October: Date Festival, Erfoud; Music Festival, Essaouira.

December: Olive Festival, Rhafsaï, in the Rif.

FOOD AND DRINK

In recent years Moroccan cuisine has begun to gain an international reputation. Not only is it a simple, varied cuisine, based on fresh ingredients such as chicken, lamb, fresh vegetables, spices and the ubiquitous *couscous*, but it is also remarkably healthy.

A traditional **first course** is *harira*, a delicious thick, peppery soup, with pulses and vegetables or meat. Other starters include *brochettes*, lamb cubes grilled on skewers; *kefta*, grilled lamb meatballs, with corander and cumin; *salade marocaine*, a salad of choped tomatoes, peppers, onions and cucumber; and *briouats*, pastry turnovers stuffed with spiced meat, rice and almonds.

Main courses are not good news for vegetarians. *Mechoui* is the most dramatic dish – a whole lamb, roasted in underground clay ovens and served with round *khobza* bread. *Tajine* is a stew cooked in a traditional conical pot, flavoured with olives, prunes or lemons. Although the ingredients vary, with a range of meat, fish and vegetables being used, the key to a good *tajine* is the long, gentle cooking. *Couscous* is the national dish, the traditional family Friday meal of semolina served with vegetable stew and mutton. Follow the Moroccan tradition and eat your *couscous* with the right hand: you roll the grains into a ball and then dip them into the sauce. A particular delicacy and a speciality of Fès is *pastilla* – thin pastry stuffed with a rich mixture of pigeon meat, almonds and cinamon, drenched in icing sugar.

Moroccan **desserts**, in keeping with most Arab countries, tend towards pastries. Honey is a major ingredient and desserts are usually very sweet. The most famous are *cornes de gazelles*, small pastry crescents stuffed with almonds and honey. There are sweet versions of *briouats*, and *griouches* are twisted strips of honeyed pastry, with sesame seeds.

Drink

It is difficult to avoid drinking **mint tea** in Morocco. Everywhere you go, from souk to sand dune, you will be offered a glass of green liquid, heavily laced with sugar.

Mint tea is more than a simple refreshment: it is a token of friendship, an offer of hospitality and being green brings good luck. Green is also the colour of fertility, a much favoured blessing for Moroccans. The extreme sweetness of the drink symbolises friendship and the wish of your host for your good health. It is

The famous Moroccan couscous, with mint tea.

considered good manners to drink at least three glasses lest you insult your host's hospitality.

Although Morocco is an Islamic country, it has some reasonable alcoholic beverages on offer. The most consumed drinks are Stork and Flag **beers**, brewed in Casablanca. Flag Special is more expensive, although it seldom lives up to its name.

The Romans first introduced the noble vine to Morocco back in the time of Juba II, and thanks to improvements made during French and Spanish occupation, Moroccan **wine** is now more than palatable. Red **cabernets** are the safest bet, but the **Gris de Boulaouâne rosé** is good when consumed very cold, and **Special Coquillages white** is a fine accompaniment for fish.

Restaurants and Cafés

For the ultimate Moroccan dining experience head to one of the former palaces in the main cities, now converted into exquisite dining rooms; here the food will be memorable, with prices to match. To really experience Moroccan food at its finest and most traditional it is a good idea to avoid the overtly tourist-orientated hotels and restaurants and instead try local establishments. The décor might not be as fancy but the food, atmosphere and good value will make up for it. However, there are many small towns and villages without a restaurant; in these cases, try a café or ask the locals where to eat.

Traditional Moroccan **fast food** is excellent. Street-side grills serve everything from soup and grilled meat and fish to goats' heads and fried testicles. It is wise to take it easy at first, until your stomach adapts to a new climate and cuisine. Also remember that during Ramadan many restaurants will close from sunrise to sunset.

Cafés are a way of life in Morocco. In every small town the café is the centre of social interaction, at least for the men of the town. The café is part of Morocco's colonial European heritage. Mint tea was first introduced to the country by the British in the 1800s, to be followed by French coffee at the turn of the century. Even today, big city cafés are akin to French-style establishments, serving *espresso*, orange juice and croissants. Many date from the 1920s, and have become institutions in their own right, such as those in Tangier where spies and Hollywood stars mingled during International rule, or in Rabat where politicians and diplomats discuss the latest intrigues.

Restaurant/Café Recommendations
Tangier
Guitta's (*Ave Sidi Mohammed Ben Abdallah* ☎ *09-937333*) Made famous in the 1920s as a place of intrigue and good food, it is worth a visit more for the atmosphere than for the European cuisine (fairly expensive).

Restaurant Africa (*83 Rue Salaha Eddine El Ayoubi* ☎ *09-935436*) A simple traditional restaurant serving good local food (inexpensive).

Café de France (*Place de France*) The most famous café in Tangiers during the International Era (*see* p.30).

Café Central (*Petit Socco*) The heart of the Petit Socco – a place rich in illicit history (*see* p.28).

Casablanca
A Ma Bretagne (*Ain Diab, Blvd Sidi Abderrahmane* ☎ *02-362112*) The most

famous French restaurant in Morocco (prices not for the faint-hearted – very expensive).

Restaurant de l'Etoile Marocaine (*107 Rue Alla Ben Abdallah, behind the market* ☎ *02-314100*) Fine Moroccan cuisine in a traditional setting – all tiles, cushions and cedar ceilings (inexpensive).

Fès

Dar Saada (*21 Souk Attarine* ☎ *05-634343*) A sumptuous ex-palace, serving traditional food to tour groups (lunchtime only; expensive).

Le Palais de Fès (*16 Boutouil Karaouiyne* ☎ *05-637305*) A carpet shop with café-restaurant above – as much for the view over Fès as for the food (moderate).

Rabat

Goëland (*9 Rue Moulay Ali Chérif* ☎ *07-768885*) French cuisine in elegant surroundings.

Le Fouquet's (*285 Ave Mohammed V* ☎ *07-768007*) Good value French and Moroccan dishes (moderate).

To enjoy Morrocan food in grand 'traditional' settings, opt for one of the restaurants housed in old mansions and palaces.

Street café, Agadir.

Café Maure (*Kasbah des Oudayas*) One of the most relaxed and fragrant cafés, at the back of the kasbah's Andalusian gardens.

Marrakech

Le Jacaranda (*32 Blvd Mohammed-Zektouni* ☎ *04-447215*) Inexpensive French fare including duck, oysters and fish from Essaouira (moderate).

Restaurant Yacout (*Sidi Ahmed Soussi, east of Jemaa el Fna* ☎ *04-440123*) One of Marrakech's most upmarket restaurants in a former palace (very expensive).

Café Glacier and **Café de la Place** (*East side of the Jemaa el Fna*) For an ever-changing view over the chaos of the Jemaa el Fna.

Café Renaissance (*Ave Mohammed V, Gueliz*)
A ninth floor view over the city of Marrakech.

Essaouira

Chalet de la Plage (*1 Blvd Mohammed V*
☎ *04-475972*) Situated on the seafront, this
popular restaurant offers seafood and local
dishes.

Chez Sam (*Port de Pêche* ☎ *04-476513*)
A pleasant restaurant hidden on the edge of
the fishing port serving shrimp, lobster, crab
and countless fish.

Agadir

Le Miramar (*Blvd Mohammed V* ☎ *08-840770*)
Good fish and pasta dishes at this straight-
forward Italian restaurant (moderate).

La Pergola (*Inezgane, 8km Route d'Agadir*
☎ *08-830841*) Good value French cooking
(moderate).

Ouarzazate

Chez Dimitri (*Ave Mohammed V*
☎ *04-882653*) One-time watering hole for
the French Foreign Legion, this inexpensive
restaurant serves unpretentious French
cooking (moderate).

Kasbah de Tifoultoute (*8km north-west of
centre* ☎ *04-882813*) Once this hotel housed
the cast of *Lawrence of Arabia*. Today it serves
traditional Moroccan food to tour groups,
with cabaret entertainment (moderate).

SHOPPING

If you want to buy anything in the souks of
Morocco, you will have to haggle. Prices are
rarely displayed and you must bargain for
any purchase – an alien and at first daunting
process for some, but one which can be fun
after a little practice.

Bargaining is simple. On seeing something
you'd like, ask the price. The merchant will
quote an exaggerated figure – often many

Carpet-seller in the souk, Rabat.

times the price he's prepared to sell it for. You then offer a price lower than the amount you are prepared to pay. The merchant lowers his price, and so on, until you both agree a final figure. Shopping with a guide may seem easier, but your purchase will be more expensive: guides receive commissions from stallholders for bringing you to their stall, which you pay as part of the final price agreed.

If you do not want to haggle, go to the local *ensemble artisanal* where you'll find a series of boutiques displaying official (more expensive) fixed prices for crafts, which can be used as a guide when bargaining. Prices in food markets are fixed, so you should not haggle over prices here.

Many visitors leave Morocco as the proud owners of a **Moroccan carpet**, but to get the best deal and a good quality carpet you should bear the following points in mind. Firstly, you should be aware of the three main types of Moroccan carpet: Rabati carpets, generally the most expensive, have

Arabic designs and Persian knotting; Berber carpets, with their striking designs and bright colours, originate in the Middle and High Atlas; and brightly coloured *kilim* are thinner rugs which are woven rather than knotted.

Secondly, it is worth visiting the officially-run *ensemble artisanal* to get an idea of prices and what to look for, before you attempt to bargain for your carpet. You should aim to pay a little less than the prices in the *ensemble*. You can watch carpets being made in factories such as the Cooperative des Tapis at the Kasbah des Oudaïas, in Rabat.

Finally, you should always check for an official label on a carpet. The State regulates all carpets with coloured labels: blue for superior quality knotting, yellow/orange for good quality and green for average quality.

Apart from carpets, there is a wealth of other good quality traditional crafts to choose from. You can always hear the metalworkers before you reach the

A worker crafting a brass plate.

workshops – the tapping of tiny hammers on **pewter** and **brass**. Huge brass plates are a favourite souvenir, along with the small silver-spouted teapots. Silver and semi-precious stones form the bulk of Moroccan **jewellery**. Berber necklaces and bracelets are the most stunning, made of heavy metal and semi-precious stones.

Moroccan **pottery** is simple, eye-catching and inexpensive, which makes it an ideal souvenir or gift. You will find many roadside stalls selling bowls, plates and urns stacked in great piles. In Fès, several boutiques sell the more expensive (and delicate) traditional **Fès blue pottery**.

Moroccan **woodcrafts** are usually very good value, ranging from the rough animal carvings of the Middle Atlas to the exquisite Thuya boxes, trays, chess sets and wooden cups of Essaouira.

Leather goods have long been a feature of Moroccan craftsmanship. Today the leather industry is still booming; jackets, cushions, slippers and wallets are all good value and usually of good quality.

It is difficult to find real **antiques** in Morocco. Fakes are common, so unless you are an expert, it is advisable to concentrate on newer goods.

Shopping Recommendations

The best places to buy crafts and souvenirs are, of course, the **souks**. Each town, and the souks within the towns, have their own specialities, where you will find the largest range and the best prices. **Rabat** is a good starting point, as the atmosphere in the medina is less frenetic. It is the best place in the country for carpets. The best pottery is found in Fès, along with metalwork and

Leather shop, Marrakech.

leather goods. In the souks of Marrakech, look for Berber carpets and spices (American visitors should note that stringent customs regulations may prohibit the import of foodstuffs into the US). Further north, the souks of Tetouan offer distinct Riffian textiles. For wood, Essaouira cannot be beaten, and the souks offer the exquisite Thuya carving of local artists.

Tangier

Galerie Tindouf (*64 Rue de la Liberté*) – antiques and curiosities; Parfumerie Maldini (*14 Rue Sebou*) – Morocco's top perfume manufacturer.

Fès

Chez Benlamlih (*75 Talaa Kebira*) – for fine metalwork; Maroquinerie Industrielle de Fès (*Rue 802, Sidi Brahim Industrial Zone*) – leather goods direct from the factory.

Rabat

Rue des Consuls – rows of carpet shops.

Essaouira
Galerie Mogador (*3 Rue de Yemen*) – young
designers show their talent with Thuya
wood.
Galerie d'Art Fredéric Damgaard (*Ave Oqba
Ibn Nafiaâ*) – painting and sculpture by
contemporary Moroccan artists.
Marrakech
La Porte d'Or (*115 Rue Souk Smarine*) –
southern Berber carpets.

ENTERTAINMENT AND NIGHTLIFE

Morocco's cultural diversity is reflected in
the range of entertainment it has to offer. As
in many Arabs countries, local
entertainment revolves around the café and
innumerable cups of mint tea, at least for
men (for women are rarely seen in cafés).
Although ostensibly an Islamic country, **bars**
are not hard to find. Moroccan bars also
tend to be the reserve of the male
population, although mixed bars are more
common in cosmopolitan cities and in up-
market hotels. Nightlife is largely centred
around tourist areas and up-market hotels,
which often offer evening **folklore cabarets**,
including belly dancing (*shikat*), traditional
dances, music and singing while you eat.
Classical music, **theatre** and **opera** can be
found in Casablanca and Rabat.

Some of the most memorable sights in
Morocco are the spontaneous **street
entertainers** found in most major towns.
Indeed, Morocco boasts perhaps one of the
last great informal open-air arenas in the
world – the Jemaa el Fna in Marrakech,
where acrobats, snake-charmers, boxers,
musicians, card-sharks and food vendors
provide a raucous spectacle that remains as

Displays of traditional belly-dancing are a standard part of the floor-shows in tourist resorts.

vibrant and impulsive as it was in the Middle Ages (*see* p.63). It is important to remember that while street entertainers seem to perform for the pleasure of it, they are in fact professionals, performing as in any theatre. You should give them money if you stop to watch the show – without payment the great traditions of street performance in Morocco will soon die out.

HAMMAMS AND SPAS

The **public bath**, or *hammam*, is a traditional mainstay of Moroccan life. Each medina *derb* (district) has its own bath-house, with water heated by the ovens in the local bakery. Men and women bathe separately (usually during the day for women, and in the evening for men, but check times locally).

Traditional *hammams* offer little more than buckets of water. Larger baths provide pools of different temperatures and massages. Although ablutions are part of Islamic religious observance, for many Moroccans a trip to the local *hammam* is also a time for meeting friends and generally relaxing after a hard day's work.

The medicinal qualities of Moroccan mineral waters were first discovered by the Romans. The Middle Atlas is the centre of **spa treatment**. Moulay-Yâcoub, just outside Fès, is the newest spa resort, while more traditional spa baths are found at Sidi Harazem, 15km (9.3 miles) east of Fès.

SPORTS

As befits a people living in a land of extreme natural beauty, Moroccans are avid pursuers of outdoor sports. **Football** (known as soccer in North America) is as much a passion in Morocco as it is in Europe and South

America, and you will come across matches almost anywhere you go. The national team is one of the best in Africa, having qualified for both the 1990 and 1994 World Cup finals.

Morocco's reputation as a growing **golfing** destination is a result of King Hassan's passion for the sport. There are now many fine golf courses scattered throughout the country, attracting top world professionals and amateurs alike. **Tennis** is a year-round sport in Morocco, and is available in major towns and larger hotels.

Morocco is a **fishing** paradise. Not only are there 2 800km (1 730 miles) of Atlantic coast and 530km (330 miles) of Mediterranean coast, but also a surprising number of inland freshwater lakes. Coarse fishing is common, with lakes and reservoirs well stocked with pike, bass and perch, in particular those east of Imouzzèr-du-Kandar, Moulay-Youssef east of Marrakech and El Kansera west of Meknès. You will need a

Taking a put at the Royal Dar Es Salam Golf Course, Rabat.

permit, available through local tourist offices. Deep-sea fishers do not need a permit. For the more adventurous, the waters off the Western Sahara are rapidly becoming known for big-game fishing – tuna and even sharks.

Birdwatchers are well served, as Morocco is a stopover on migration routes each spring and autumn, and also hosts many interesting breeding species, including Morocco's national bird, the white stork. Good places for birdwatching include the lakes of the Middle Atlas, and the valleys of the High Atlas. The northern coast is good for migrating species, and there is a bird reserve at Sidi Bourhaba (25km/15.5 miles north of Rabat).

Morocco's sparsely populated countryside attracts hunters from round the world. Moroccan **hunting** reserves boast fine grouse, fowl and wild boar. Hunting reserves are usually run by travel groups, who can arrange temporary import licences for guns.

As one of the most mountainous countries in Africa, Morocco is an excellent place for **hiking**. The High Atlas, Middle Atlas, Anti-Atlas and Rif ranges all offer well-established hiking trails. Even the highest mountain in North Africa, Mount Toubkal, can be hiked up rather than climbed (*see* p.72). The ideal time for hiking in the High Atlas is from April to October. Snow blocks many routes in winter. The Toubkal Massif south of Marrakech is the most popular destination and is easily accessible. Less explored regions include the Azilal Massif, to the south of Beni-Mellal, and the towering Irhil M'Goun range – the second highest in Morocco, accessible from Ouarzazate. Furthest east, the Midelt Massif, fringed with cedar forests, offers some of the best and least-known hiking in the country.

Spring and autumn are the best seasons for walking in the Middle Atlas. The western limestone plateau from Khenifra to Ifrane boasts twisted rock formations and oak and cedar forests populated by Barbary apes. To the east is the more rugged Massif of Taza, including the National Park of Tazzeka. It is often a good idea to hire a guide to show you trails. Mules can also be hired to carry baggage. Note that guides do not work during Ramadan.

The mountains of Morocco offer plenty of other sports too. **Mountain biking** is developing in Morocco, centred on the trails of the Middle and High Atlas. Take your own bike or rent from companies in Marrakech and Fès. It may come as a surprise, but you can **ski** in Morocco. The country's top resort is Oukaïmeden, in the High Atlas, open from December until April. The second resort, Mischliffen, in the Middle Atlas, is open for six weeks each winter. Off-piste skiing is possible in the High Atlas – you hike to 4 000m (12 800ft) summits, with your skis carried on mules, then ski down to the bottom.

Many new companies offer **four-wheel-drive tours** of desert and mountain areas. Contact local travel agencies or large hotels for details. However, the classic way to see the desert is by camel. Numerous operators run **camel treks** to the edge of the Sahara, lasting from a few hours to a couple of days, exploring the oases and sand dunes. The two main bases for camel treks are in the Ziz and Drâa valleys. Hotels in Merzouga, near Erfoud, can arrange trips to·the massive Erg Chebbi dunes, while Zagora in the Drâa valley offers tours to the dunes of Tinfou. More sedate camel trips are available on Agadir beach.

If horses are more your style, you will not be disappointed: **riding** has long been a Moroccan tradition. Riding holidays are available in the Anti-Atlas and Middle Atlas, or you can simply hire a horse and guide from local hotels. Alternatively, **mule treks** can be arranged in most hill villages. In the High Atlas, trips can be arranged from Setti-Fatma, Ouirgane, and Imlil. In the Middle Atlas, Ifrane and Azrou offer mule treks.

Sailing, water skiing, jet-ski, sub-aqua diving, and paragliding are just some of the **watersports** offered along Morocco's long coastline. Agadir is the watersport capital of the country, while Mediterranean resorts offer more gentle water activities. Morocco is also a surfing and windsurfing utopia: Essaouira is a renowned windsurfing destination, while surfers skip the waves at Taghazout near Agadir, Plage des Nations at Rabat, and Mehdiya.

Mountain biking in the High Atlas – taking a break at the Glaoui kasbah of Taourirt.

THE BASICS

Before You Go

Citizens of Australia, Canada, Europe, New Zealand, the Republic of Ireland, the UK and the US (plus several other countries) do not require a visa for stays of less than 90 days, but they must be in possession of a full passport that is valid for at least six months after the date of entry into Morocco. Children under 16 may travel on the passport of the person accompanying them as long as a photograph of the child is attached to the passport.

Vaccinations are not required for visitors arriving from Europe or America. Travellers from areas where cholera is present may be required to produce an anti-cholera vaccination certificate. It is recommended that vaccinations for polio, tetanus, typhoid and hepatitis-A are kept up to date, especially for those travelling independently in rural areas.

Getting There

Morocco's main airport is at Casablanca, through which most international flights pass, and there are also direct flights to Marrakech. Connecting flights are available to Agadir, Fès, Ouarzazate and Tangier.

There are some direct flights to Tangier. Royal Air Maroc (RAM), Morocco's national airline, provides the most regular flights from major cities in Europe (including London), North America and the Middle East.

If you want to drive to Morocco, head for Algeciras in Spain from where regular car ferries operate to Tangier (2½ hours) and Ceuta (1½ hours). Ferries also operate from Sète in France to Tangier – a

crossing of 36 hours.

It is possible to get to Morocco by rail from many cities in Europe. For example, by changing at Madrid it is possible to get from Paris to Algeciras in 24 hours. From the airport at Casablanca regular train services operate between the airport and Casablanca and Rabat.

Warning

Despite the widespread availability of kif (hashish) in Morocco, it is illegal to sell or consume kif. You should not let yourself be pressured into buying kif (which may also be called 'chocolate') from persistent street dealers. It is not wise to linger in the main kif-production areas of the Rif mountains, where there are police roadblocks and those caught possessing drugs are not treated leniently.

Typical oasis.

A-Z

Accidents and Breakdowns

Accidents should be reported to the traffic police (*Sureté nationale*). If you are in a hired car, the rental firm should be able to help with breakdowns, so carry their details with you at all times.

Airports see Getting There, p.112

Babysitters see Children

Banks

Banks are generally open from 8-11.30am and from 2-4pm, Monday to Friday. The exchange rate is fixed by the government so there is little competition between the banks. Banks in the larger towns have cash dispensers (ATM) where you can withdraw money using international cards.
See **Money**

Beaches

The beaches on the Mediterranean coast are more sheltered and far safer for swimming than those on the Atlantic, where there are strong offshore currents and brisk breezes. Only swim on those beaches where recommended. That said, the Atlantic has some fine stretches of sand with excellent opportunities for surfing and windsurfing, and Agadir and Essaouira are excellent for

Sail-boats on the beach, Agadir.

more energetic watersports. Along the Mediterranean coastline sailing is very popular, especially around Al Hoceima. Nude sunbathing is not permitted on public beaches.

Bicycles
Mountain-biking can be fun around Marrakech. Some of the more upmarket hotels offer bicycles for hire.

Books
In 1931 Paul Bowles accompanied Aaron Copeland to Tangier. There Bowles wrote his famous novels *The Sheltering Sky* and *The Spider's House.* Such was the power of Morocco over him that he never left. His experience inspired the writers of the 'beat generation' to follow his path. Allen Ginsberg, Jack Kerouac and William S Burroughs (whose *Naked Lunch* is set in Interzone, a warped version of Tangier) all spent time in Morocco. Playwrights Tennessee Williams and Joe Orton were also drawn there.

One of the most entrancing books on the country is Elias Canetti's *The Voices of Marrakesh*, a novel about Jews in the mellah of Marrakech. *Morocco – The Traveller's Companion*, Margaret and Robin Bidwell's compilation of literary writings about Morocco, and *In the Lap of Atlas*, Richard Hughes' collection of traditional Moroccan stories, make interesting reading. For those able to understand French, *The Memoirs of King Hassan II* are fascinating.

Breakdowns *see* Accidents

Buses *see* Transport

Camping
Camping and caravanning are possible all over Morocco, with well over 80 officially recognised sites located in the most popular tourist areas of the country. Many are close to beaches along the Atlantic coast. All very reasonably priced by European standards, the sites offer facilities which vary from rudimentary to sophisticated. Camping elsewhere requires the permission of the landowner. A full list of campsites is available from the Moroccan National Tourist Office (*see* **Tourist Information**).

Car Hire
The minimum age for hiring a car is 21 (there may be a supplement to pay if you are under 25) and you must have

held a full driver's licence for at least a year. Most of the international car hire firms are represented in Morocco and there are also a number of local firms. It is advisable (although not compulsory) to take out collision waiver damage and personal accident insurance. Make sure the tyres, including the spare, are in good condition and check the brakes and lights before driving the car away.

Children

Families visiting Morocco tend to opt for the coastal resorts (the beaches on the Mediterranean coast being safer for children, *see* **Beaches**) rather than the cities. Many of the coastal resort hotels cater specifically for children, and many water- and beach-based activities are readily available. Some of the bigger hotels offer a babysitting service, and smaller hotels will often make arrangements.

The busy streets of the cities with their noisy souks are not very suitable for young children but in Marrakech horsedrawn carriages called *calèches* are a good compromise (establish the price before setting off). A ride on a camel or mule, either along the beaches or into the hills, makes a good diversion for older children.

Pharmacies are well stocked with European brands of the day-to-day requirements of babies.

Churches see Religion

Climate see p.88

Clothing

What to take depends whether you are visiting the northern or the southern half of the country, the coast or the mountains (*see* p.88). When it is hot, light cotton clothing is best but evenings can be cool. When in the desert, the temperature difference between day and night can be extreme. Generally, dress should be modest (shoulders, upper arms and legs covered) when away from the beach *See also* **Etiquette**

Complaints

In the first instance, always try and settle a problem with the manager of the establishment. If this fails, ask for the complaints book; the law requires that all hotels and restaurants have one. If your complaint is still not dealt with satisfactorily, seek advice from the nearest tourist office.

To avoid any potential unpleasantness, always establish the price of something in advance so there is no misunderstanding, particularly when dealing with taxi drivers and guides.

Consulates

Embassies and consulates can be found at the following addresses:

Australia *see* **UK**
Canada 13 Bis Rue Jaafar as-Sadik, Rabat ☎ 07-672880
France 3 Rue Sahnoun, Agdal, Rabat ☎ 07-777822
Ireland *see* **UK**
New Zealand *see* **UK**
UK (Australia, Ireland, New Zealand) 17 Blvd de la Tour Hassan, Rabat ☎ 07-720905
US 2 Avenue de Marrakech, Rabat ☎ 07-762265

Crime

Violent crime is rare in Morocco, but sensible precautions should be taken against the risk of petty theft.

• Carry as little money, and as few credit cards, as possible, and leave any valuables in the hotel safe.
• Carry wallets and purses in secure pockets or wear a money belt, and carry handbags across your body or firmly under your arm.
• Cars are often targetted, so never leave your car unlocked, and hide away or, better still, remove items of value.
• Beware of drug trafficking and never accept or agree to carry packages from strangers. Nor should bags ever be left unattended, particularly at airports.

Currency *see* **Money**

Customs and Entry Regulations

Personal effects can be freely taken into Morocco but alcohol is restricted to one bottle of wine and one bottle of spirits per adult, and the limit on cigarettes is 200, or 50 cigars or 250g of tobacco.

Restrictions apply to arms and ammunition for hunting (shotguns are prohibited) and professional photographic equipment.

Dirhams can only be exchanged in Morocco (*see* **Money**).

Disabled Visitors

There are few special facilities for disabled travellers and many places, such as the crowded souks, will be difficult to get around. Some of the more expensive modern hotels, however, provide good facilities for disabled people, and several have lifts. Information can be obtained from the Moroccan National Tourist Office or travel agents.

Long-haul Holidays and Travel is available from RADAR, 12 City Forum, 250 City Road, London EC1V 8AF, ☎ 0171 250 3222 (open from 10am-4pm). It contains advice and information about accommodation, transport, services, equipment and tour operators in many countries, including Morocco. The Holiday Care Service is available to advise British disabled people wishing to travel abroad, and can be contacted on ☎ 01293 774535.

Driving

Cars drive on the right-hand side in Morocco and vehicles approaching from the right have priority. It is compulsory to wear both front and back seat belts. Driving conditions are usually quite good, but potential hazards are children, mopeds and horse-drawn carts, who pay scant regard to traffic regulations.

Motorists driving their own car in Morocco should carry with them a full driver's licence, an international motor insurance certificate, a green card and the vehicle's registration document.

Speed limits are as follows:
• motorways: 120kph/75mph
• built-up areas: 40-60kph/25-38mph
• other roads: 100kph/63mph

Roadsigns are in Arabic and French. In most towns and villages, parking is controlled by attendants who require a small fee (variable) of a few *dirhams*. In return, they will keep a eye on your car and perhaps clean the windscreen.

Petrol is easy to come by on the main roads but away from these it is wise to fill up whenever you pass a station. Apart from in large towns, unleaded (*sans plomb*) petrol may be difficult to get.

Dry Cleaning see Laundry

Electric Current

The current is 220V in all new buildings but in older ones 110V may still be in use. Sockets are the round, two-pin variety so you will need an adaptor if you are taking your own appliances.

Embassies *see* **Consulates**

Emergencies
Police ☎ 19
Fire Service ☎ 15
Ambulance ☎ 15
Highway Emergency Service
☎ 177

Etiquette
As is always the case when
visiting a foreign country,
awareness of and respect for
local customs is important.
Traditionally, Moroccans are
friendly and hospitable.
• In general, although there
are a few exceptions, access to
mosques and other holy places
is forbidden to non-Muslims.
• When away from the beach it
is important to dress modestly,
with shoulders, upper arms
and legs covered. This is
particularly so for women and
also discourages unwelcome
attention.
• If you want to photograph a
person, ask their permission
first and do not press the point.
• Try to be as discreet as
possible about eating, drinking
or smoking during the day
throughout the month of
Ramadan, when Muslims forgo
these pleasures entirely
between dawn and dusk.
• If you are offered a cup of
mint tea, accept politely as it is
a sign of hospitality.

Traditional musician.

Excursions
When visiting a Moroccan
town the medina (old town) is
usually the first port of call and
this area can be explored on
foot. Tourists will be
approached by many would-be
'guides' (including children),
all clamouring for your
attention. If you decide to
choose one of them, be sure to
establish the price at the
outset, but it is probably better
to stick to the official
Moroccan Tourist Ministry
guides who are recognisable by
their uniform and badge.
These guides can be found
outside large hotels and at the

regional head offices of the National Ministry of Tourism.

Large hotels and travel agents can advise about local tours and excursions.

Guidebooks see **Maps**

Health
There is no free health care for visitors to Morocco, so comprehensive medical insurance should be taken out in advance. To avoid upset stomachs, be sure to drink only bottled or boiled water (don't forget ice cubes and cleaning your teeth), steer clear of salads (unless you are sure it has been thoroughly washed in purified water) and fruit (unless you peel it yourself), and be wary of food from street stalls.

It is advisable to take with you a first-aid kit containing anti-diarrhoea tablets, water purifiers, disinfectant and sun tan cream (even in winter). Pharmacies, however, stock most European medicines. *See also* **Water**

Hours see **Opening Hours**

Information see **Tourist Information Offices**

Language
The official language of Morocco is Arabic, but most Moroccans speak French as well, and many speak Spanish (particularly in the north) and English too. Moroccan Arabic, as widely spoken, differs quite considerably from classical written Arabic. Although no-one will expect you to speak Arabic, if you can master at least one or two basic expressions, it will be well received. Here are a few useful phrases:

Hello (informal) **Labes**
Hello (formal) **As-salaam 'alaykum**
Goodbye **Beslamah**
Please **Minfadlik**
Thank you **Choukran**
Yes **Waha**
No **La**
How much? **Bsh hal?**
Too expensive **Ghalee bzef**
Where is...? **Fayn kayn...?**

Laundry

There are no self-service launderettes in Morocco, but getting clothes washed is rarely a problem as practically all hotels, however simple, provide a laundry service.

Lost Property

The best course of action is to inform the hotel desk or the local tourist office who will be able to advise, and if necessary call the police for you.

Maps

The Michelin sheet map 959 will enable you to plan your routes if touring Morocco. The *Michelin Green Guide Maroc* (French edition only) contains information on the towns, sights and main attractions of the country, together with maps, street plans and background information.

Medical Care *see* Health

Money

The official Moroccan unit of currency is the *dirham* (dh), which is divided into 100 *centimes*. Notes come in denominations of 10, 50 100 and 200 *dirhams*; coins in 1 and 5 *dirhams* and 5, 10, 20 and 50 *centimes*. Occasionally prices may be quoted in *rials*, common currency (rather like

Cranes, Tangier.

the erstwhile French *sous*) in the souks. In effect, this unit is worth one twentieth of a *dirham*.

Dirhams can only be obtained in Morocco and are not exchangeable outside the country. When changing money into *dirhams* you will be given a slip which you will need to keep and present if you wish to change any money back into your own currency at the end of your stay.

The best place to change money or travellers' cheques is at a bank, an official change office or the larger hotels: the rate is fixed by the government so the rate varies very little from place to place. Never change money in the street as this is illegal.

Credit cards are widely accepted in larger hotels and many restaurants, but cash is obviously your best bet when bargaining for purchases. In larger towns, money can be withdrawn from cash dispensers (ATM) with international credit cards. *See also* **Banks**

Newspapers

British newspapers and the *International Herald Tribune* are generally available a day or two after publication. Even more widespread are the French dailies. Locally produced French-language publications include *Le Matin du Sahara* and *L'Opinion*.

Opening Hours

Shops generally open between 8.30am-noon and from 2.30-7pm, with food shops staying open until 8/9pm. Outside the medina, shops tend to be closed on Saturdays and Sundays and during the major religious festivals. The souks (markets) are closed on national holidays but stay open on Sundays. On Fridays, the day of solemn prayer, a good many shops stay closed and less business is conducted, but the main tourist areas are likely to carry on almost as normal.

Offices: Business hours are Monday-Thursday 8.30am-noon and 2-6.30pm, Friday 8.30-11.30am and 3-6.30pm.
Museums: These are generally open every day except Tuesdays and Friday afternoons. Opening hours vary, but are around 8.30-11.30am and 2.15-4.30pm.

During the sacred month of Ramadan the daily way of life in Morocco is subject to various changes that are worth noting. Opening hours of shops, monuments and museums tend to be restricted, particularly in smaller towns, as are train and bus services. Commercial activity also tends to be transferred from the day to the evening, so many businesses open their doors late into the night instead. *See also* **Banks** and **Post Offices**

Photography

The major brands of film are widely available in the towns and resorts of Morocco, and many photo shops offer a 24-hour (or less) processing service. The light is extremely bright in Morocco so suitable film should be used.

Remember to keep cameras and film out of intense heat and sunshine, and take care to avoid sand and dust getting into equipment.

If you want to take photographs of people outside tourist areas, always ask their permission first and don't press the point if they are reluctant. Street entertainers and sellers will expect a small tip for being photographed. When visiting museums and other public buildings, look out for any restrictions on photography.
See also **Customs**

Police

There are two police forces in Morocco, the civil police, the *sureté nationale*, and the military *gendarmerie*. The *sureté nationale* wear grey uniforms with a white belt and white flat cap, and are responsible for tourists. Their emergency number is ☎ 19. Most towns have a police station.

Post Offices

Post Offices (PTT) are open from 8.30-11.45am and from 2.30-6.30pm, Monday to Friday. In large towns, they are open all day. *Poste restante* mail should be addressed to the main post office of the nearest city.

Stamps can be purchased at post offices (but be prepared for long queues), tobacconists (*tabacs*), hotel reception desks and tourist shops.

Public Holidays

These fall into two categories in Morocco – official secular holidays and religious holidays. The latter follow the lunar calendar and therefore change every year.

Official Holidays

New Year's Day: 1 January
Independence manifesto: 11 January
Feast of the Throne: 3 March
Labour Day: 1 May
National Day: 23 May
Young People's Day: 9 July
Allegiance of Wadi-Eddahab: 14 August
Anniversary of the King's and People's Revolution: 20 August

Anniversary of the Green
March: 6 November
Independence Day:
18 November
Religious Holidays
Aïd el-Fitr (marking the end of
the four weeks of Ramadan)
Aïd el-kebir (commemorates
Abraham's sacrifice)
First of Moharram (Muslim
New Year)
Mawlid an-Nabi (celebration of
the birth of the Prophet
Mohammed)

Public Transport see
Transport

Religion
Morocco is a Muslim country
and the official religion is
Islam. There are very few
Anglican churches in Morocco,
but Roman Catholic churches
are fairly widespread. Jewish
synagogues can be found in
the larger cities.

Smoking
Smoking is acceptable in most
places and at most times in
Morrocco. However, this is one
of the pleasures foregone by
Muslims during Ramadan, so
foreigners should refrain from
smoking in public in daylight
hours during this period.

Stamps see **Post Offices**

Taxis see **Transport**

Telephones
Telephone calls can either be
made from a telephone cubicle
inside a post office where
payment is made at the end of
the call at a central desk, or
from phone boxes on the
street which take both coins
and cards. Phone cards are
available from post offices (see
Post Offices) and some
tobacconists and kiosks.
Phoning from hotels, although
convenient, is very expensive.

   To make an international
call, dial ☎ 00 followed by the
country code, followed by the
STD code (minus the initial 0)
then the subscriber number.
To call within Morocco, dial
the six-figure number if within
the same area; if calling from
one area to another, dial the two-
digit area code first (02 to 09).
International information:
☎ 12

Information: ☎ 16
Country codes are as follows:
Australia: ☎ 0061
Canada: ☎ 001
Ireland: ☎ 00353
New Zealand: ☎ 0064
UK: ☎ 0044
USA: ☎ 001

Time Difference

Morocco time follows
Greenwich Mean Time (GMT)
all year round, so during the
summer it is one hour behind
the UK and six hours behind
the eastern US.

Tipping

It is a good idea to have plenty
of small change in your pocket
at all times as guides, waiters,
porters, petrol pump
attendants and parking
attendants (*see* **Driving**) expect
a tip for their services. Hotel
bills include a service charge,
as do restaurant bills, but
waiters still expect an extra 5-
10 per cent as a tip. Taxi
drivers do not expect a gratuity
if the price of the ride has
been agreed beforehand.
Beware of handing out *dirhams*
too readily to appealing
children, as you will be followed
by a clamouring horde.

Toilets

Apart from those in modern
hotels and restaurants, toilets
in Morocco may come as a bit
of a shock to westerners. More
often than not they are the
hole-in-the-ground variety and
there is no toilet paper. Lack of
water and the intense heat do
not help either.

Tourist Information Offices

In most towns in Morocco you
will find a branch of the
Moroccan National Tourist
Office or a tourist information
bureau.
   Moroccan National Tourist
Offices abroad:
Australia: 11 West Street
North, Sydney NSW 2 060
☎ 02-922 4999
Canada: 2001 Rue Université,
Suite 1460, Montreal H3A 2A6
☎ 514-842-8111
UK: 205 Regent Street,
London W1R 7DE
☎ 0171 437 0073
US: 20 East 46th Street, Suite
1201, New York 10017
☎ 212-949-8184

Tours *see* **Excursions**

Transport

RAM offers several domestic
flights to most of the major
cities and has ticket offices
where reservations can be
made in all the country's main
centres. Prices are relatively
cheap and it is well worth
considering travelling long

distances by air.

Although Morocco's railway system is concentrated in the north of the country and coverage is not extensive, the express trains are fast, comfortable and air-conditioned; first and second class seats are available. Some main cities are not served by rail but the National Railways (ONCF) provides bus connections. For information ☎ 07-774747.

Buses are a popular means of transport in Morocco and as a result it is usually necessary to book seats in advance. CTM is the main company, running comfortable, air-conditioned coaches ☎ 02-448127. Various small private 'companies' exist but they are less reliable.

In town centres, the *petits taxis* (maximum three people) are cheap and reliable. They are a different colour in each town – red in Casablanca, blue in Rabat, and so on. Other passengers going in the same direction can be taken on board too. A meter should be in operation but if for any reason it is not, settle the price at the outset.

Grands taxis (maximum six people) will take you to the suburbs or to other towns. Unless you want to pay for the empty seats, the driver will wait until his car is full.

TV and Radio

The larger, more expensive hotels usually have satellite television receiving CNN and Sky, plus some other channels. The local channels broadcast in Arabic, but the news and several other programmes are also repeated in French.

The BBC World Service can be obtained on short wave; local stations, all in Arabic, provide a range of music, news, sport and current affairs.

Vaccinations *see* Before You Go, p.112

Water

It is advisable never to drink (or clean your teeth with) anything other than bottled or boiled water, and avoid ice cubes because they will have been made from tap water. Before swimming in a wadi or a lake, particularly in the south, take advice as to whether it is safe as bilharzia is prevalent.

What to Wear *see* Weather, p.88

Youth Hostels *see* Accommodation, p.89

INDEX